Michael Kilgarriff is an experienced actor, comedian, old time music hall chairman, cabaret artiste, author and – standing six feet six in his socks – in strong seasonal demand as a pantomime giant. ('He's got very tall socks,' is how Harry Secombe introduces him.)

By the same author

THE GOLDEN AGE OF MELODRAMA
MAKE 'EM LAUGH
IT GIVES ME GREAT PLEASURE

Compilations

1,000 JOKES FOR ALL OCCASIONS
1,000 JOKES FOR KIDS
BEST SHOWBIZ JOKES
BEST LEGAL JOKES
BEST BOSS & WORKER JOKES
BEST FOREIGNER JOKES
BEST TEENAGER JOKES
BEST SERVICE JOKES
MORE BEST RELIGIOUS JOKES

Sketches

THREE MELODRAMAS
THREE MORE MELODRAMAS
MUSIC HALL MISCELLANY

Michael Kilgarriff

Comic Speeches For All Occasions

... And How To Make Them

Futura
Macdonald & Co
London & Sydney

A Futura Book

First published in Great Britain by
Futura Publications Limited in 1978
Reprinted 1981, 1984, 1985

Copyright © 1977 by Michael Kilgarriff

TO JOHNNY

ISBN 0 7088 1460 3

Printed in Great Britain by
Hazell Watson & Viney Limited,
Member of the BPCC Group,
Aylesbury, Bucks

Futura Publications
A Division of
Macdonald & Co (Publishers) Ltd
Maxwell House
74 Worship Street
London EC2A 2EN
A BPCC plc Company

Contents

Preface

Speechmaking is quite a simple business.

First of all, you must tell everyone why they are there. They already know, of course, but they like to have a formal, ritual, public pronouncement of the assemblage's title and purpose.

Then talk about the people present who will be familiar to the majority – personalities are much more interesting than abstractions. And as we are concerned with comic speeches, when you have decided whom you are going to mention – be rude.

Finally ('. . . but seriously, folks . . .') spread a thick layer of sentimentality over the gathering. When a group of people with a common interest have put on their glad rags and come together to eat and drink and reassure each other of their identities and importance and place in the firmament, they will accept any amount of mawkish gush. I have omitted these slushy endings from the speeches herein partly in the interest of my digestion and partly because you can't expect me to do *everything* for you, can you?

I said that speechmaking is simple, but I didn't say that it was easy, so in the Introduction I shall attempt to analyse the problems in greater detail.

Making a speech is terrifying enough, but to make a comic speech you need iron nerve, unshakable confidence, immaculate timing, style, delivery, good diction, etc., etc. You have none of these qualities and attributes? Never mind, laddie. You have something the others don't have; you have *this book!*

Michael Kilgarriff
Ealing

Introduction: How to deliver a speech

If you've got to make a speech you might as well be audible, so let us consider voice production first of all. This is a highly complex and technical subject, rendered even more obscure by the failure of teachers to agree on the best method. It is well established, however, that a voice (whether spoken or sung) is best produced from the 'stomach' rather than the 'throat'.

I've put these two words in inverted commas because I use them more in a metaphorical than a literal sense. By speaking from the 'throat' I mean uttering in the normal everyday manner; if the voice, used in this way, is raised it becomes a shout, which is unpleasant to listen to and fatiguing to the speaker. When people become hoarse or lose their voices, it is because they have been shouting, i.e. speaking or singing loudly from the wrong 'position' – again I must resort to those tiresome inverted commas, since 'position' here means not how you stand but how you *place* your voice.

To speak (or sing) from the stomach requires more of a psychological approach than an actual physical one, and how to achieve this aim is where authorities differ. I should interpolate at this point that the vocal techniques of speaking and singing are not exactly alike, as anyone who has heard professional singers trying to speak dialogue will know, but for our purposes the difference is immaterial.

Speaking from the stomach means utilizing not the throat, which will do its work unconsciously, but the rib-cage and the diaphram. Imagine that your voice is coming from the pit of your stomach and not from your larynx: this is the essence of what is called projection. Try it in the privacy of your own home (send the wife and kids out first) and you will immediately feel and hear a change.

The tone and quality of your voice depend on many things; practice being one, but also considerations like your sinuses, the size of your tongue and the interior of your mouth, the contours of your hard and soft palates, the configuration of your pharynx, nasal cavities and Eustachian tubes, and even, to some extent, your height. So I am not trying to show you how to achieve the voice beautiful in one easy lesson, but simply how to make yourself audible without shouting. In practical terms this means keeping plenty of air in your lungs and 'thinking' an open throat.

Posture

Stand up straight. This will give the appearance of confidence, even if your kneecaps are trembling, and will seek to reassure your audience that you are in charge not only of yourself but of them. With your back straight, your vocal apparatus also has the best chance of functioning properly. Keep still – i.e. don't shuffle your feet or over-gesticulate – and speak in your mind's eye to someone in the back row; this will give you a semblance of authority and help to ensure that you are heard.

This question of authority is very important. I have just referred to your being in charge of an audience. This is just what the great entertainers achieve, of course, in that their audiences are quite happy to be taken in hand, so to speak, and led where the performer wishes them to go. I well remember after I had taken the chair one evening at the Players' Theatre in Charing Cross, where there is a lengthy tradition of heckling the chairman. An actor friend of mine who had been in the audience said to me, 'You know what I like so much about seeing you in the chair? You are so totally in command; we are all quite confident that you'll never be thrown.' Naturally I took this as a splendid compliment, particularly as I was sick with apprehension before the show.

So don't lean on the table or lectern, keep your feet and your hands still and your back straight. What you need, in a word, is repose.

Gesture

I have already warned twice about the dangers of over-gesticulating. Nothing gives away a state of funk more readily than a speaker's restless hands and arms; if you wish to hypnotize your audience then by all means semaphore like a demented windmill, but if you do your audience will (a) be unable to attend to a word you utter, and/or (b) be reduced to giggles.

Leave the stabbing finger and the clenched fist to the politicians – these gestures are as much clichés as 'at this point in time' or 'make no mistake about it'. I do a great deal of speaking in public and hardly ever raise my hands; if yours worry you, stuff them in your trousers. (This may seem a touch unmannerly but at least it will give the appearance of casualness.) If you happen to be a female and therefore without trouser pockets, just hold your hands loosely before you. You can also clutch your notes, of course, but if you are nervous they will tremble like aspen leaves in a Force Ten gale, so it is best to leave them on the table if you can see that far.

If you need glasses for reading, by the way, I think it is far better to leave them on after each consultation of your notes. You may complain that to leave them on will detract from your beauty and make your audience dissolve into a vague blur. To which I would reply that a slight diminution of your personal charms is a small price to pay to avoid the extreme irritation of seeing you constantly taking your specs on and off; and for your audience to melt into a blur may well be an advantage from your point of view – that way you won't see them fidgeting and yawning.

Timing

Timing is an inborn sense of rhythm. It tells you when to stop and when to start and you either have it or you don't. There is no golden rule about timing; some people speak very slowly and others very quickly, and both may tell the same joke to equal effect. Jack Benny and Robb Wilton

11

were masters of the former technique and Bob Hope and Ted Ray of the latter. I don't think it would profit you much for me to dilate on timing, other than to advise you to watch a comic or speaker whom you admire, and whose style you feel approximates your own, to see how he or she does it. Not that you will want to give an impersonation when you get on your feet, but all comedians (and all practitioners of all art forms for that matter) are prepared to admit to 'influences'. Frankie Howerd and Max Miller have always been my gods above all stand-up patter men, but I have yet to be told that I remind anyone of these supreme artistes – I'm sorry to say . . .

The other aspects of timing are (a) when, and (b) how long. The time of your speech will not usually be in your control, since there will probably be a dinner to eat first and a chairman to introduce you. But if it is a less formal occasion, my advice would be to watch the alcohol intake of the assemblage. Let them take on board just enough to make them mellow and responsive to your prepared witticisms, but not enough to lose inhibitions and treat you as an Aunt Sally. If there is no dinner to be eaten, I would say that an hour to an hour and a quarter is as long as you want to leave it before you speak.

Never, never make a speech unless you are asked to do so. The situation may arise where you are not sure whether you will be asked to make a speech or not, in which case you will of course prepare your utterance but you will on no account deliver it unrequested. I heard only the other day of a wedding reception which was quite spoiled by a man who, to everyone's surprise, stood and made an impassioned political speech which was as embarrassing as it was irrelevant.

Now for how long. None of the speeches in this book is more than ten minutes in length. You are not delivering a Reith lecture but endeavouring to entertain without boring; ten minutes is quite long enough, and if you only speak for half that time or even less, nobody is going to complain. You will in fact be soundlessly but nonetheless gratefully thanked by those who, having taken a few drinks, will have discovered just after you have launched into your oration a pressing need to visit the washroom. This may seem a trivial, if not downright crude, observation to make but it is in fact an extremely important and practical consideration. If it is in your power you should actually attempt to arrange for a brief watering interval after coffee, say, or the Loyal Toast so that those being spoken at may listen without mounting discomfort.

So when you practise your speech in the privacy of your own boudoir, check the timing with a reliable watch. If you run over ten minutes, prune and prune until you are under the magic figure. Very few books, plays or films cannot be improved by cutting, and I am sure that your speech will be the same. If you get a lot of laughs you may well run a lot longer than you estimate, but no matter – while they're laughing you're winning.

Try to go out on a big laugh if you can, and if you find that your penultimate – or even ante-penultimate – joke gets a yock, cut it there and sit down. Don't feel that because you have prepared more you are in honour bound to speak it all: finish on a crest and then get into the cabaret announcement or dancing or whatever.

Content

I would suggest that the important consideration under this heading is relevance, which may seem a fairly unnecessary observation to make until you remember the incident already quoted of the political diatribe given at a wedding reception. Generally speaking you need to tell your audience what they want to hear, i.e. if they are greengrocers you will tell them what a lot of honest, hard-working fellows they are; salt of the earth, friend of the housewife, backbone of the country, etc., etc.

Common sense should also tell you what to avoid. At a temperance function it would be insane to crack jokes about drunks; at a farewell party you would not crack jokes about airplanes crashing or ships sinking; to a gathering at which a number of clergy were present you would do well to eschew blasphemous gags, while weddings are not the occasions to tell mother-in-law jokes or blue jokes – especially not the latter with all the mums and aunties present, not unless you want to have everyone frozen with embarrassment.

I know you want to be funny but try to write yourself a speech and not a patter act. The gags should appear to flow quite naturally, even inevitably, from the gist of your remarks. All the best comics strive towards this effect; they seem to be just chatting to us, inviting us to enter their individual world with the laughs emerging quite effortlessly and spontaneously, and you should aim for the same effect.

Try to avoid saying, 'That reminds me of a story I heard the other day'; personalize your stories, i.e. rather than saying, 'This chap went into a pub and there was a bloke at the bar who said etc. etc.' you should say, 'I went into The Grapes the other night, and old Harry Clamper was propping up the bar as usual, and he said etc., etc.' Everyone knows The Grapes and everyone knows old Harry Clamper – in fact as you say his name all eyes will turn in his direction (especially if you indicate where he is sitting at the same time) – so however silly the anecdote to follow you are more than halfway to a big laugh.

When addressing an organization or club, a quick humorous run-through of the past year's activities and achievements will always go down well, especially if you concentrate on personalities. 'I see Charlie Staircase has won the first prize again : must cost him a fortune in bribes' – this is the kind of simple, artless gag which a convivial group will always appreciate.

Beware a similar but serious review of the year by another speaker; whoever speaks first will cut the ground from under the feet of the second, so try to avoid duplication of material by checking with the Secretary concerned, or even with the other speaker or speakers themselves.

A comic history of the group you are addressing is another possible peg on which you hang your speech, i.e. 'This Society was founded in 1167 by Edric the Eccentric while on a Crusade to the Holy Land . . . he was on a day excursion to (*local*) actually . . .' Instead of Edric the Eccentric you might introduce the nickname of someone on the top table, and the day excursion could be to the local night-club or gambling den or naughty district. And you could finish a speech on this theme by looking into the future.

Keep it light and frothy with plenty of pace, without gabbling and without fidgeting.

I was going to say that!

The public speaker's nightmare is hearing the previous speaker using his best gag. You can surreptitiously shuffle through your notecards under the table and score through the joke with your sweaty ballpoint, desperately thinking of an alternative, but what if the joke is the lynch-pin of your whole speech? All you can do is to improvise, giving your audience the simplest, shortest and straightest speech it will ever have been their pleasure to listen to.

One precaution to take if feasible is to check your jokes with the other speaker or speakers beforehand; if two of you have the same witticism planned it will need a little tact on your part to persuade the other chap that you *need* the gag, whereas he with his vast experience and enormous repertoire will be able to find a replacement without having his evening ruined.

If you think this is going to be sticky, try to ensure that the chairman or responsible official of the club or organization is present – he will have invited you both to speak and so presumably will know you both well enough to mediate. I have had to adjudicate in this way myself more than once with professional comics, and have usually found that one will be prepared to cede without any fuss.

And what if you find that the previous speaker is exhibiting a comedic talent that would bring a standing ovation at the London Palladium? * Instead of feigning a

* I have had the pleasure of appearing in three productions at this great theatre, without, it must be admitted, eliciting anything in the nature of an ovation. In fact, to be brutally frank, I was booed

15

heart attack so that you can be carried out, you speak as follows:

'Ladies and Gentlemen,

(*Name of the speaker*) and I were chatting at the bar just before dinner, and he confessed to me that he was very worried about having to address you tonight because, on arriving here, he found that he had lost his speech. He seemed so upset and distraught that I thought I'd make the big gesture – so I gave him mine.'

And on that you sit down. Believe me, you will get as big a reception as Mr. Personality did before you. Resist all attempts to get you back on your feet; anything further can only be an anti-climax.

Noisy audiences

If there is a lot of noise while you are speaking it is tempting to try and make yourself heard over it; the experienced speaker knows that the trick is to get *quieter*. The noise-makers will soon be shushed by their better behaved neighbours, but if the chatter gets worse and worse and even starts spreading you might as well face the fact that you've lost your audience so cut to the peroration and sit down quick.

To the dread cry of, 'We can't hear you!' there are various responses. 'Well, you'd better bloody well shut up, then!' may be all right in some circles, but they are not the ones in which you or I would care to mix. A better response might be, 'Can't you hear me at the back?'

And then to the predictable reply of 'No!' you wittily riposte, pointing to your ears, 'I'm not surprised – most people hear at the side!'

This should get you a good laugh and maybe even a sympathetic round of applause. But it's even better if you don't permit the situation to arise. My standard comment to a group of chatterers is to stop, look at them and say,

---

and hissed. But then the Giant in pantomime mustn't expect to get too many laughs, must he . . . ?

'I'm so sorry – am I interrupting your conversation?' This gets a very good reaction, rather better than 'I'm sorry – I couldn't hear you. I was talking.'

If a table is persistently and aggressively noisy there isn't a lot you can do about it. 'What's up – no school tomorrow?' or 'I wish your mothers would come and take you home,' may get the audience on your side and demonstrate to the rowdies that their efforts to ruin your speech are not being appreciated, but if they are drunk there is no way of cowing them. Take it from me that a party of drunken men (and drunken women are even worse) is no audience for a speech, so cut your losses and sit down.

Microphones

With a microphone in your hand things are easier. But there are mikes and mikes. Some can safely be left on the table or stand to pick up your every whisper, others merely give out a buzzing echo even when pushed right down your trachea. If you have to use a mike – and as most people have become stone deaf over the past ten years you almost certainly will – try to ensure that there is a competent person in charge of the controls *at all times*. Remember the principle that if something can go wrong it will, and microphones are high on the list of probables in this respect.

It is usually better to speak over a mike rather than straight into it; this way you will avoid popping your f's and p's and distortion will be minimized. But even with a mike a little more effort is required than for the ordinary conversational level of speaking. Before his retirement I frequently worked for the distinguished BBC radio drama producer Archie Campbell,* one of whose frequent comments to actors during studio rehearsals was, 'More binge, please – a little more binge', which might be defined not as mere volume but as edge, positiveness, body.

* That I worked for him frequently has, of course, nothing to do with the fact that I married his secretary.

Pace

With or without a microphone you want to be intelligible as well as audible, so you must speak slower than your normal pace. You know what you are saying but your audience doesn't, it takes time for them to hear what you have said, assimilate it and then laugh at the joke, if joke it was.

How much slower should you speak? That really depends on the size of the hall and the size of your audience. The further away from you they are the longer the reaction will take, as is shown by the phenomenon well known to actors that laughter almost always begins at the front stalls and rolls away backwards and upwards. Politicians' speeches, when delivered to a large audience in a large conference hall and then viewed in close-up on television in your own home always seem to be slow and over-emphatic. But the speaker has adjusted to the size of the auditorium and the number of his auditors; a smaller audience in a smaller room would require a corresponding scaling down of gesture and delivery.

Lighting is a factor worth considering. Perhaps it isn't always appreciated that audiences to a large extent lip-read; if you can't be seen too well you'll need to allow for this by speaking even more slowly and distinctly.

There are many other aspects to public speaking such as acoustics, phrasing, diction, inflection, etc., etc., but as long as you are heard and get your laughs and don't go on too long – who cares?

Practicalities

Don't write out your speech in full. Only an experienced public speaker can make a written speech sound spontaneous, so just jot down your headings (I have indicated these after each speech) on cards – not scraps of paper. And don't forget to number the cards in sequence. Filing cards are the right size, with three entries on each one.

Now, using the cards, run through what you have planned to say two or three times, but don't rehearse too

18

meticulously or you'll sound stilted and unnatural, adding to the general embarrassment. The only parts of your speech that should be practised until you have eliminated all the stumbling, hesitating or fluffing are the funny stories. Your speech won't suffer too much if your quick cracks and one-liners are mis-timed or otherwise muffed, but a story with a plot and a boffo tag-line needs a certain amount of work and care.

Take care also with your headings. Make them instantly intelligible to yourself – how often have you sat writhing in boredom while a speaker tries to interpret his own notes? Take the opportunity afforded by a big laugh to look at the next one: if you write them in capitals with a felt pen you won't have to peer and mumble to yourself. Another tip: during your speech, you will probably be in a none-too-composed frame of mind, so when you look at your headings you will probably blurt out whatever you have written. For this reason it is generally best to make your headings the first few words that you actually *intend* to say. You'll see what I mean when you practise.

Finally, if you miss a heading, it is fatal to go back. You will lose your thread, your flow, and in trying to leapfrog you will just get yourself in a dreadful muddle. No, if you miss a heading, just leave it – it was probably better omitted anyway.

To summarize

BEFORE
1. Prepare in detail
2. Write your headings legibly and intelligibly.
3. Practise
4. Time the length of your speech

ON THE NIGHT
1. Pick your moment (where practicable)
2. Stand up straight and keep your feet still

3. Speak slowly, clearly and loudly without shouting.
4. Keep the gestures to a minimum
5. Sit down while you're ahead

And in conclusion

Try not to worry too much. After all, you're not addressing a plenary session of the United Nations, so don't give yourself an ulcer worrying about what is after all a perfectly commonplace social event. Your audience will probably be largely acquainted with or related to you, so the worse that can happen is a little friendly badinage, which is all to the good. And if your audience are all strangers and the occasion an important and serious one, you shouldn't be attempting a comic alloquy in the first place, should you?

The ensuing speeches are intended primarily as guides or frameworks. Adapt them, shorten them, lengthen them (but not too much!), substitute your own stories – in short, alter them freely to suit your own personality. After all, I am not you and you are not me, so what I can get a laugh with you might not. With which morale boosting remark I shall end these helpful comments and leave you to wallow in an ecstasy of stage fright. One old professional dodge, incidentally, in dealing with 'butterflies', and one which is surprisingly effective, is to take a few deep, slow breaths just before you start.

Finally, have a couple of stiff Scotches first, they'll do you more good than anything I might suggest . . .

But before I sit down

In order to give you full value for your money all the openings, closing and contents of the ensuing speeches are completely different; very few of the jokes, quips, cracks or one-liners are given more than once.

I am only too aware, therefore, that you may not find exactly what you require under the relevant heading, but if you look through some of the other speeches I am sure you won't fail to find material suited to your precise needs.

1

Annual Dinner: General

This first speech is analysed in detail to give you some idea of how the effectiveness of a speech may be maximized; subsequent speeches will just indicate pause for laughs by suspension dots, with notes after the suggested headings.

SPEECH	ANALYSIS
	Stand up straight and fear-lessly; speak immediately you rise.
Ladies and gentlemen – and those of you from the despatch department –	*Slight pause*
	Speak this as an after-thought. Mention here any department notorious for its inefficiency or rudeness or any other shortcomings. Or it can be a department known for its rivalry to your own. Wait for the cheers to
I won't keep you long – I want to get through before the pills wear off –	*subside*
	This is a big laugh so give it air
and we have dancing tonight to (*name of band leader*) and his Adur Estuary Stompers,	*The band's description should be altered to suit. Other suggestions are given in later speeches; if, however, the musicians are full-time professionals not locally known it is better to give them a straight introduction*

so I'll keep it short.

Did you enjoy the dinner?

at the appropriate time cutting this reference. Run this line straight on after your band gag. Wait for the response – mostly your audience will say 'yes' but there are always one or two wags who will shout 'no'. If the 'no' shouts are loud enough you can speak 'it should be good' in a tone of surprise.

It should be good – I checked in the kitchen this afternoon and ten thousand flies can't be wrong.

This is a big laugh

Now then, once again the Annual Dinner/Dance of the (*name of club or organization*) has come round and in the past year a lot has happened. Yes, since last June

Alter to suit

We've all passed a lot of water – no! –

Alter to suit

Speak the 'no!' quickly as though you've only just realized what you've said

I mean, a lot of water – oh, forget it. For instance, (*name*) has had a rise –

Wait for reaction. Try to ensure that any names you mention will be recognizable to the majority of your audience. Getting roars of mirth from one solitary table doesn't do much for the rest of those present, and they may even begin to resent having to sit through a lot of private in-jokes. We all know how irritating it is when radio disc jockeys persist in telling us about the lady who has just brought in the coffee, or how Jim in the control room is laughing, so do your best to make all your references generally intelligible.

they've moved his office to the next floor up . . .
And then (*name*) has been made a director –

Pause for laugh
Choose someone very unlikely
there may be a good reaction here, to which you can reply 'what do you mean – never?' getting another laugh

– he's now directing people to the car park

If there is no car park you could say that he is now directing people to the gents, or to somewhere equally unsalubrious in the building.

Poor old (*name*) has had the plague,

This will be a reference to someone who is now happily recovered

and (*female name*) has had a baby!
Will the proud father kindly rise?

Wait for reaction

Here by prearrangement you will have organized six or seven men dotted around the room to stand up on cue. Wait for the reaction to subside a little and then say:

We'll really have to tear up her Red Rover

Or local equivalent. Or 'we'll really have to let the air out of her tyres' or 'lock her bike away'

In my own department

24

things are moving –
my spare chair's been nicked
for a start!

Pause for laugh

Still, we have got a
computer now. Not that I
can work the damn thing,
mind you –

Slight pause.

I'll never get the hang of all
those beads.

Pause for laugh.

But further news: it is
strongly rumoured that as
soon as (*name*) can steel
himself to

*This will be a hirsute, trendy
young man.*

buy a new suit

*Or coat or tie or bike or
whatever.*

he's also going to have a
shave and a haircut!
I used to have a beard
myself once, you know, but
then one day I thought I'd
have it off –

*Pause for laugh.
If you have a beard, say,
'Do you like my beard? I
was thinking of having it
off . . .' Give the audience
time to take in the rude
implication of this line.*

– it was the wife's idea,
actually –

Pause for laugh.

so I went to my barber, he
was a West Indian chap as it
happened, and I said to him:
'Can you give me a shave?'
He said, 'Yaas,' I said,
'No – just my chin.'

Pause.

*Speak this very fast, and then
look puzzled, muttering, 'I
wonder why he said that?' to
yourself. This is a very big
laugh, and you needn't
worry about upsetting any
West Indians in your
audience. I have told this gag*

countless times, and believe me when I tell you that coloured people laugh at it as much as anyone.

But it's really marvellous to see such a good turn-out again on such a cold night.

Pause to let your audience agree

On my way here I passed three brass monkeys looking distinctly worried.

Speak this rapidly. If it is hot, you can say: 'on my way here I saw a tree chasing a dog,' which is a bigger laugh than you might expect.

No, really, as your president I'm very gratified at the turn-out. I'm not so sure about (*name*)'s turn-out, but then he / she always did go too far.

Or chairman or whatever.

This will be another trendy youngster, who could be a female showing off a good deal of her charms.

Our Hon Treas – he's such a treasure – tells me that most of you have paid for tonight, so (*name of lady committee member*) and I won't have to do the washing-up again this year.

Don't wait for a laugh on this quip.

This should be someone grand, like the wife of the managing director.

(*Name*), your Hon Sick – Sec – I'm so sorry –

This to be said as though it was a slip of the tongue. Don't wait too long, but depending on the personality involved it could be a big laugh.

wanted to read the minutes of last year's thrash, but as we've only got an extension till two o'clock

Alter to suit. If there is no extension you can say, 'but the last bus goes at three in the morning'.

we'll take them as read.
Actually, I've seen them and
they're not so much red as
blue. I didn't know some of
you carried on in (*name*)'s
flat afterwards ...
and carry on's the word!
Still, chacun à son goût,
which roughly translated
means Jack's got the gout.

*This will be a well-known
raver of either sex.*

*This is best if you have a
Jack on the top table you
can refer to. If not, an
alternative might be: 'Still,
sic transit gloria mundi,
which roughly translated
means Gloria should be all
right by Monday' on which
you will cross your fingers
and look despairingly at the
ceiling.*

As you may know, we're
doing our bit towards
Britain's exports, and in fact
we've gone into a new line
entirely. We've started
selling coffee ...

*Expect a puzzled reaction on
this.*

It's true, didn't you know?
Our first overseas customer
was a German firm, but this
venture hasn't been going
altogether successfully,
because after we sent them
our first two shipments we
received the following letter :
'Mein Tear Herren,
Der last two pecketches ve
got from you off coffee was
mitt rattschidtten mixt. Ve
did not see any rattschidtten
in der samples vich you sent

*You will need to write this
out and actually read it. If it
is not suitable for the
occasion, you could use the
Apology for Absence letter
on page 42.*

27

us. It takes much valuable time to pick de ratten durden from der coffee. Ve order der coffee clean but you schipt schidt mixt mit it.

Your audience will take a little time to catch the drift of this gag. Take your time, however, and don't panic. The first big laugh comes on 'but you schipt schidt mixt mit it' and from then on you are away. You must of course use a strong German accent without making yourself incomprehensible. If you can't do this satisfactorily I would again refer you to the Apology for Absence letter. Don't worry about this gag offending.

Ve like you schip us der coffee in vun sek, und der rattenschidtten in an udder sek –

Pause.

und zen ve can mix it to suit der customer,

Another big laugh.

Write, blease, if we should schip der schidt bek und keep der coffee,

Speak this rapidly, then pause.

or should ve chip bek der schidt und schip der coffee bek.

Speak this rapidly also and pause again.

or should ve schip bek der whole schidtten vurks? Ve remain at your conwenience . . .'

A very big laugh.

Fold the letter up and replace it in your pocket. You should get a round of applause on this one, out of which you can say:

28

My mother told me that

*Or 'the chaplain' or 'Mrs.
Whitehouse' or anyone in
the firm who might suit.*

Apologies have been
received from (*name*), who
unfortunately can't be with
us tonight – he's helping the
police with their enquiries.

*This could be a genuine
absentee.
Pause for giggle.*

Perhaps he's the one who
nicked my chair . . . ?

Just a throw-away.

Also (*name*) can't be here –

Another genuine absentee.

He's languishing in a
sick-bed . . .

Pause.

his girl friend's got flu.

*If this is a newly-married
man you can use the name
of his wife, i.e. 'Linda's got
flu'.*

Be that as it may, I know
you'll be delighted to learn
that in honour of this
sus – auspicious occasion

*This is a cod slip of-the-
tongue. If it gets a laugh
(which isn't all that likely)
you can say, 'I'm breaking
these teeth in for the day'.*

drinks will be entirely free!

*Wait for cheers to subside.
If the reaction is small, say
'what's the matter – are you
all teetotallers? Drinks will
be entirely* free!*' This will
definitely provoke the
response you require.*

However . . .

*Pause for your audience to
have time to appreciate that
there is going to be a
let-down.*

a nominal charge will be
made for the use of the
glasses.

*Say this quite slowly but
with a grin.*

There is, by the way, a wild and wicked raffle this evening, with tickets now available from our dolly birds. You can tell which are our girls – they've got the firm's name stamped on their left ... elbows.

Obviously you will let your audience momentarily think you are going to say 'left breasts'.

Be generous, since all the money raised tonight will tomorrow morning be going straight to – Messrs. Barclays Bank.

Speak this quite seriously. Or 'on Monday morning'. Pause for effect. This usually gets a big laugh. Use your imagination for local variations, e.g.:

The prizes are magnificent: the first prize is a week's holiday in the Rotherhithe Tunnel. The second prize is two weeks' holiday in the Rotherhithe Tunnel ...

Brighton:	*Hove*
Cardiff:	*Penarth*
Edinburgh:	*Tour of Sir Walter Scott Memorial Camping Holiday on Arthur's Seat*
Glasgow:	*Govan*
Liverpool:	*Mersey Tunnel*
London:	*Cruise on Hackney Marshes or*

	Brentford Reservoir
Manchester:	*Mancunian Way*
Nottingham:	*Mortimer's Passage*
Oxford:	*Rollright Stones*
Wolverhampton:	*Smethwick (& vice versa)*
Worcester:	*Redditch*

Also usable in this context are Stonehenge, Eddystone Lighthouse, The Goodwin Sands, Spurn Head, Gateshead, Middlesbrough Transporter Bridge, local crematorium, cemetery, abattoir, etc., etc.

Well, now, the bottom of my glass is distinctly damp, so I'll finish by saying how nice it is to see you all – or most of you –

Show your glass to be empty as you speak this.

Here you can glare at a rowdy party

again, and now : on with the dance

You will have arranged with the band-leader to strike up on this cue. Or, if you have to introduce another speaker, say:

Well, now, you've enjoyed yourselves long enough, so your kind attention please for the next speaker . . .

a man whose charm, talents and looks have made him a much-loved figure to us all;

give this quip time to sink in speak this slowly and sincerely.

31

he is also the man who wrote
this introduction, Mr.
(*name*)!

*Get the name in before the
laugh on 'the man who
wrote this introduction' has
time to swamp you; this way
you sit down and the next
speaker rises on laughter
and applause. It would be
tactful if you warn the next
speaker that you are going to
take the mickey, which will
give him the chance to think
up a rejoinder.*

Suggested Headings

Despatch department.
Won't be long. Pills.
Name of band and gag.
Enjoy meal? 10,000 flies.
Once again Annual Dinner/Dance. Passed water.
(*Name*) has had rise – moved office to floor up.
(*Name*) made director – car park.
(*Name*) has had plague, and (*name*) a baby. Father rise?
In my dept. things are moving – spare chair nicked.
Computer – beads.
Rumoured that when (*name*) buys new coat he'll have a
shave and hair cut.
I used to have a beard. West Indian barber.
Good turn-out on cold night. Three brass monkeys.
(*Name's*) turn-out.
Hon. Treas. say most have paid – no washing-up
with (*name*)
Hon. Sick – Sec. to read minutes, but extension till 2.00.
Minutes not red but blue. Carry on in (*name's*) flat.
Chacun à son goût.
Exports. Coffee. Rattschidt letter.

Apologies for absence. (*Name*) helping police – nicked my chair?
(*Name*) languishing in sick bed.
Drinks entirely free.
Raffle. Tickets from dolly birds stamped on left elbows.
Money to Barclays Bank.
1st prize: week's holiday in (*local*).
2nd prize: two weeks' holiday in (*same*).
Bottom of glass damp, so on with the dance!

2

Annual Dinner: Old Boys' Reunion

I won't keep you long . . . (*wait for cheers to subside*) . . . I want to, er, water the horses . . . anyway, enjoy the meal? (*wait for response*) Anyone got any bicarb? (*hand over stomach and wince*) Now then, are you all enjoying yourselves? (*wait for response*) . . . why – what are you doing?

It's marvellous to see such a turn-out on a cold night like this. When I got on the bus to come here I was frozen – I'd been waiting for the best part of half an hour – so I said to the conductor, 'My goodness me, my feet are like ice!' He said, 'Yes, man, an' mine are like choc ice!' [1]

. . . But it is also nice to see you making your annual attempt to look smart and presentable . . . I always have such a terrible time with my tie, don't you? By the time I got here it had come undone again, so I asked one of the waiters to help with it. 'Certainly, sir,' he said, 'lie down.' I said, 'Lie down?' He said, 'Yes, if you please, sir.' So I lay down flat on a sofa in the lounge and he did my tie up – beautifully, as you can see. I said to him, 'Why did you want me to lie down?' He said, 'That's the only way I can do them, sir. I used to be an undertaker.'

(*Point to man with bald head sitting nearby*) Would you mind moving? The light from your head is shining in my eyes . . . that's the only bright spot in my speech . . . as I said, I won't keep you long – I must be home before eleven or the wife lets out my room.

I have to announce a little disappointment for you: we were to have had a special cabaret attraction – The Dance Of The Three Virgins . . . but unfortunately . . . they've broken their contract. Still, (*name*) has promised to sing Largo Al Factotum while drinking a pint of beer, so all is not lost? [2]

Now, to some more news: we'd like to welcome home (*Name – see gags in Welcome Home speech on page 242*).

(*Name*) has passed his finals and is now a fully paid up member of the Inland Revenue . . . (*Name*) has just got the concession at Battersea Power Station (*or local reference*) . . . (*Name*) has just taken possession of a new suit from John Collier. He always wears John Collier's clothes – I wonder what John Collier wears? It's made from virgin wool, he tells me. That's wool from the sheep that runs the fastest . . .

Then we'd like to congratulate (*Name*), whose wife has just presented him with a precious little bungle – bundle. And (*name*) of course has a new wife. Never mind, the first five years are the hardest, if you'll pardon the expression. I think his wife's going to have a rough time, poor girl. I wouldn't trust him with a double-breasted jacket . . .

I was at the wedding, as it happened. At the reception I said to the best man, 'Where's the happy couple, then?' He said, 'They're upstairs putting their things together.' His mother-in-law's a trial, though. She was thrown out of the Mafia for cruelty. She's in show business – just come back from a very successful season at Loch Ness.

Which reminds me of one of us present – I won't say his name – but he's been having marital troubles. One night while they were in bed his wife burst into tears and said, 'I have a confession to make – I've been to bed with another man.' He said, 'So have I – turn over!'

Then poor old (*name*) has been crossed in love. He was crazy about this girl, said he'd follow her to the ends of the earth . . . I can just imagine it, can't you? . . . and he would have done, too, but she moved to (*local neighbouring town, or unsalubrious area*). Mind you, I think he had a lucky escape – she was so ugly! Had a face like a bag of chisels – she couldn't have her face lifted so she had her body lowered.

Which brings me to my wife – she'd been in a bad mood lately. She's taken to wrapping my sandwiches in a road map . . . I got in late the other night and said, 'Sorry I'm late, darling. Is my dinner still hot?' She said, 'It should be – it's been on the fire since seven o'clock.'

Her mother's been staying with us . . . her mother: what

a man! When I told her I wanted to marry her daughter she went up the wall! 'You marry my daughter!' she said. 'You! You're effeminate!' Me – effeminate! Mind you, next to her I am.

She's been staying with us because she's broken her leg. It's all done up in plaster and the doctor says she's not to go upstairs – and the racket she makes climbing the drain-pipe at bedtime . . .!

Still, the old school is progressing well. Last year's results are up to scratch: 38 'O' levels, 14 'A' levels, and 15 street levels. The local Schools Inspector came round, so I was told, and when he visited Class Four he asked them to give him a number. One of the boys called out, 'Twenty-seven!' so the Inspector wrote seven two on the blackboard. Nobody said anything, so he asked for another number. 'Forty-eight!' someone shouted, so he wrote eight four on the blackboard. And again nobody said a word. For the third time the inspector asked for a number. 'Thirty-three!' came a shout, at which a small voice from the back of the class was heard to say, 'Let's see 'im make a balls-up of that one!'

I remember the inspector coming round once during Mr. (*history-master*)'s lesson. He pointed to (*name*) and said, 'You, boy! Who signed the Magna Carta?' And (*name*) burst into tears and said, 'Please, sir, it wasn't me!'

Our cricket team ended the season well. I was watching our last match when the spectator next to me said, 'What a rotten bowler – what a rotten bowler!' I said, 'I'm sorry – it's the best I could afford' . . . I only played once or twice myself, not too successfully. The last time I was batting, the umpire – he must have been wearing his glasses *over* his contact lenses – gave me out. I said, 'What for?' He said, 'For the rest of the afternoon!' . . .

Our football team: it has been decided in future that the National Anthem will be played *before* each match – that's to make sure they can still stand up . . . but still, they have had bad luck. I was present on the notable occasion when the ref was awarded a free kick. 'Who for?' asked (*Name of captain*) and the ref said, 'Us' . . .

The finances of the club are in the customary parlous state. Our treasurer tells me there's hardly anything left in the kitty, but he did enjoy his month in the Bahamas . . . the sub will have to go up again, I'm afraid. Either that or the beer consumption will have to double . . .

In aid of club funds, we are having a raffle tonight. Buy lavishly, gentlemen, if you please. The first prize is a 10lb jar of rat poison, and a year's free supply of rats.

But nevertheless, the club is going from strength to strength, which is more than can be said for the beer. That reminds me, there will be a free pint for everyone here – yes, a free pint with every 50p bag of crisps . . . but you don't want to drink too much of the stuff here. You won't get so much drunk as waterlogged . . . besides, it does terrible things to the sheets . . .

I'll finish now – we're having a beer-drinking competition and I want to see who's coming in second, so will you all please charge your glasses, rise and drink to: The Club!

Suggested Headings

Water for the horses.
Enjoy the meal? Bicarb.
Enjoying yourselves. What are you doing?
Good turn-out on cold night.
My feet are like ice.
Terrible time tying my tie. Undertaker.
Bald head shining.
Back before eleven.
Dance of Three Virgins.
(*Name*) to sing Largo Al Factotum while drinking pint.
Welcome Home to (*Name*).
(*Name*) has passed finals and now fully-paid up member of Inland Revenue.
(*Name*) has got concession at Battersea Power Station.
(*Name*) taken possession of new suit from John Collier. Virgin wool.
(*Name*) precious little bungle.
(*Name*) new wife. First five years hardest.

Wouldn't trust with double-breasted jacket.

At reception. 'Upstairs putting their things together'.

Mother-in-law. Thrown out of Mafia for cruelty. Back from season at Loch Ness.

Wife's confession. 'Been to bed with another man.'

(*Name*) has been crossed in love. Girl moved to (*local*).

Ugly girl – face like a bag of chisels.

Couldn't have face lifted but had body lowered.

My wife in bad mood. Sandwiches in road map.

'Is dinner hot?' 'On fire since seven'.

Mother-in-law staying. Effeminate.

Broken leg. Racket climbing drainpipe at bedtime.

Schools Inspector.

School progressing well. 38 O levels, 14 A levels, 15 street levels.

    'Twenty-seven'. Wrote 72.

    'Forty-eight'. Wrote 84.

    'Thirty-three'.

    'Let's see him make a balls of *that* one!'

'Who signed Magna Carta?'

Cricket. Rotten bowler.

I was given out. 'What for?'

Football. Play National Anthem before each match.

Ref awarded free kick. Who for? Us.

Finances of club in parlous state. Treas says nothing left but he did enjoy his month in the Bahamas.

Sub going up or beer consumption must double.

Raffle. 1st prize; 10lb jar of rat poison and a year's free supply of rats.

Club going from strength to strength. Not beer.

Free pint with every 50p packet of crisps.

Don't drink too much. Waterlogged. Sheets . . .

Finish: having beer-drinking comp. I want to see who comes in second.

Toast. The Club!

Notes

1. This of course to be said in West Indian accent.
2. This might well be altered to include any member present who is well known for any unusual hobby or job, i.e. Charlie will give us a quick cantata on his organ, *or*, Harry Black (*a dentist*) will show us how he does an extraction blindfold and with one hand tied behind his back, *or* Jim Walsh will hypnotise Sandy McGregor into paying for a round, *etc., etc.*

The 'items of news' regarding members present can be extended indefinitely. Other suggestions might be:

(*Name*) always wanted to be a sex maniac, but he failed the medical.

(*Name*) wanted to be a donor for artificial insemination but the competition was too stiff.

(*Name*) couldn't be here tonight – he's been refused bail.

(*Name*) has become a Corporation dustman. £12 a week and as much as he can eat.

(*Name*) is a meteorologist. He can look in a girl's eye and tell whether . . .

(*Name*) has become a stripper. As soon as we've finished he'll be on the roof stripping the lead off.

3

Annual Dinner: Social Club

Good ladies, evening and gentlemen – I mean, good evening, ladies and gentlemen – I knew I should have practised this speech. Did you all enjoy the meal? I didn't have the tomato soup myself, the chef's a vampire. Anyway . . .[1] As vice-president of this club – and who better than myself to be in charge of vice? – (*A voice from the hall shouts 'Hear, hear!'*) Where? Where? Oh, I see . . .[2] yes, well . . . it falls to my lot to give you a short address, and here it is:

42, (LOCAL) High St.

I've paid for these jokes and I'm going to use 'em . . .[3]

Well, now, here we are again. Another scintillating, sparkling annual bunfight unparalleled in the annals of the (*name of club or society*) since (*name of recently married member*)'s stag party last month. He's still working off the damages every Saturday night in the kitchen . . .

Now then, our regular attenders at this annual do will know – and I trust we're all regular? Are we all regular? (*wait for shouts of 'Yes!'*) Anyone who isn't see me afterwards and bring your own spoon . . . regular attenders will know that it is customary for me to give you an annual report . . . BANG!

New members will be delighted to know that this year's president[4] is a man of substance. His grandfather was a peer . . . and his grandmother had kidney trouble as well, poor old thing . . . Still, our finances are to remain in the capable hands and sticky fingers of (*name of treasurer*). I am happy to say that our bank balance is in a healthy state, so we shall be able to make our usual annual donation to the (*name of prominent wealthy member or local notable*) Benevolent Fund. Well, he needs it, poor chap – he's just given his third footman a rise.

Our social events were looked after most efficiently by (*name*). He does have a slight complaint about you all, though. He told me that he was a trifle hurt as being called 'Droopy Drawers' by some of the younger members. I told him not to be upset – it was just in fun. 'I know that,' he said, 'but it shows which way the wind's blowing' . . .

Our annual fête was as usual a fête worse than death – NO! – it was of course as ever a rousing success, and we have to thank Mrs. (*name*) and her intrepid band of helpers for the refreshments. We would also like to thank Dr (*name*) for his professional services afterwards. I was told that at the fête, by the way, Mrs (*name*) [5] went up to (*name of prominent member or celebrity guest*) and said, 'I haven't told you about my grandchildren, have I?' And he said, 'No, you haven't madam, and I'd like you to know how deeply I appreciate it!'

We should further like to thank our Hon Sec, (*name*), who slaves all day long over a hot secretary on our behalf. He told me he went into Smith's the other day. There was a lovely girl behind the counter, and he said to her, 'Do you keep stationery?' She said, 'No, I wriggle a bit.'

Our stalwart bar steward – you have to be careful how you say that – bar . . . steward [6] also deserves our thanks. Mind you, he does slip up from time to time. I remember last month I was in the bar and ordered a pint. I took one sip – not good at all. 'This pint's bad,' I said. 'You should worry,' he said, 'I've got six barrels of the muck in the cellar!' [7]

But he has his problems. There was that barmaid we had for a short time last March – remember her boys? What a super superstructure! And the low-cut blouses she wore – whew! I'd seen nothing like it since I was weaned. But she had to go – (*name of steward*) said she kept dipping in the till . . .

Nor must we forget our loyal porter, known to us all as Billiard Cue Charlie. We call him that because he works better with a tip.

Then I'd like to thank our committee on your behalf, ladies and gentlemen. So often with organizations like ours half the committee does all the work while the other half does nothing at all. I am happy to say that with our committee it's the complete opposite.

I mustn't leave out the Mayor of (*local*) without whose help this evening would almost certainly have happened, and finally I'd like to thank my parents for having me.[8]

Apologies for absence have been received from – well, I'd better not say who, but it is one of our lady members who wrote to me as follows : (*reading*)

'Dear Mr. (*name*)'

I much regret that I shall not be able to attend the dinner/dance on Friday. This is because of my hubby, who simply will not let me alone. He just wants to make love to me all the time . . .' Lucky for some . . . 'No matter what I am doing in the house – washing-up, ironing or cleaning, he just keeps on' (*turn the page over and then turn back*) 'keeps on. So I am sure you will understand why I cannot be with you. Yours sincerely, etc., etc.

PS Please excuse the wobbly writing.'

Well, now, I want to see a man about a dog – the retiring rooms are at the back by the way. Ladies on the right and gentlemen on the left. If you get them confused it may be embarrassing but think of the friends you'll make.

For your cabaret tonight we have Lord Privy and his Performing Seal . . . and we also have the shortest Indian Fire Walker in the world – Singhis Thing. For your dancing pleasure we couldn't afford a disco so we've hired Sid Shortwind and his oversextette, better known and feared throughout the country as (*name of band*).

But first of all, may I ask you to rise for the loyal toast. OR So let the orgy commence!

Suggested Headings

Good ladies, evening and gents. Should have practised.
Enjoy meal? No tomato soup. Chef's a vampire.
As vice-president.
Give you a short address.
Another scintillating, sparkling annual bunfight.

Are we all regular? Annual Report.

This year's pres a man of substance. Grandfather was a peer.

Finances – (*name of treasurer*). Annual donation to (*name*).

Social events (*name*). Droopy Drawers.

Annual fête a fête worse than death.

Thank (*name*) for refreshments.

Thank Dr (*name*) for his professional services afterwards.

Mrs (*name*) went up to (*name*). Grandchildren.

Hon Sec. Slaves over hot secretary. Stationery.

Stalwart bar steward. Careful how you say it. 'Beer's bad'.

Barmaid with super superstructure. Kept dipping in till.

Porter. Billiard Cue Charlie.

Thank committee. So often half does all the work while the other half does nothing.

Mayor of (*local*) without whose help.

Thank parents for having me.

Apologies for absence. Read letter.

See man about a dog. Ladies on R gents on L.

Lord Privy and his Performing Seal.

Shortest Indian Fire Walker. Singhis Thing.

Couldn't afford disco. Sid Shortwind and his over-sextette.

Loyal Toast / Let the orgy commence!

Notes

The essence of a speech like this is to play up personal characteristics. Don't be afraid of offending anyone – the more outrageous your remarks the louder the laughs, and the object of your shafts won't dare to take umbrage for fear of being thought a bad sport. For instance, if you refer to someone who is prominent in the furniture business, you will refer to him as being a 'totter'; a bookmaker can be the 'only man I know with suede roller-skates'; a property developer can be a 'jerry-builder'; a nurse 'queen of the bed-pans', a priest 'a wonderful preacher – we didn't know what sin was till he came to our parish,' and so on and so on. Or you can just refer to someone as being 'well-known in concentric circles'.

43

1. If there wasn't tomato soup on the menu, alter this to 'We were going to start with tomato soup but the chef's a vampire'.
2. 'Hear, hear!' from the audience must of course be pre-arranged.
3. Repeat '42, (local) High St . . . short address . . . get it?' laughing yourself.
   This will get a giggle, but 'I've paid for these jokes etc' will then get a big laugh.
4. The name of the office can be altered to suit.
5. This will be the name of a lady renowned for boring the pants off everyone with stories about her children. Or it could be altered to a male member who has recently become a father, and who gets out the family snapshots at the drop of a hat. It is important only to use this kind of reference if you can reasonably expect most of your audience to catch the significance.
6. Bar steward can of course be made to sound like bastard.
7. Through this gag use your bar steward's name.
8. You can refer here to your local MP or any notable who is not in fact a member.
   A slight pause after the word 'would' helps this quip.

4

Annual Dinner: Sports Club

Thank you. And in conclusion . . . I'm so sorry, but like you I want to get this speech over, because as soon as I've finished the drinks are going to be free . . . (*wait for reaction to subside*) . . . providing you stick to water . . .

Well now, we've had a good year, I'm happy to say. Our membership drive is going well – we've driven six new members away this evening alone – and I'm happy to see such a good turn-out . . . television must be lousy tonight . . . hands up all those who've been to these annual meetings before? . . . (*wait for hands to rise*) . . . hell, aren't they? [1] But it's good to see you all looking respectable, even if it's only once a year. I saw old (name) beforehand resplendent in his new suit, so I said, 'you're looking smart.' He said 'Yes, I got this suit backing a horse. I backed it through Burton's window.'

Oh, before I forget (*producing a piece of paper*), will the owner of car registration number 579 WPX 2734 HUP 945 ZSQ 382 MBR (*pause for breath*) 543 MAI 9338 SAL 226 WKO 190 BBC 684 ITV 263 NGB please move his car as the number plate is blocking the driveway?

But I must tell you about a funny dream I had the other night. I dreamed that (*name*) had died . . . aaah! . . . but when he told St. Peter who he was St. Peter said, 'you're not (*name*) of the (*name of club*) are you?' (*Name*) admitted that he was, and St. Peter said, 'but you're surely not *the* (*name*). the champion (*give sport*) player?' And again (*name*) said yes he was. 'Thank goodness you've come,' said St. Peter, 'we're playing hell tomorrow.' [2]

I regret to say that our finances are not in the greatest shape – unlike (*name of club's glamour queen*), so we're going to raffle (*name's*) new car/suit/set of golf clubs/sweater to raise funds.[3]

I'm sorry that (*local dignitary*) can't be here – he's been refused bail, but I would like to mention (*name of celebrity present*).[4] I promised him I'd put one of our beauties on his right hand at dinner and another on his left hand. He said that'd be fine as long as he didn't get gangrene in his fingers. He told your committee, by the way, that they were a set of addle-pated, boring, incompetent nincompoops, which is why we're making him a Life Member.

We are all, I suppose, dedicated to the ideal so succinctly expressed in the Latin phrase 'mens sana in corpore sano'.[5] I also speak Yiddish and gum arabic, by the way. 'Mens sana in corpore sano' means, as I am sure you all know – even you (*name of club idiot*) – means a sound mind in a sound body.

It is Juvenal's ideal then that this club strives for, though when I look at the list of prize winners I don't think we're getting very far. Look at our football team – the last time they played both teams were so bad the referee was elected man of the match.

Then there's our tennis champion, (*name*). A fine player, I grant you, but anyone who can drive a motor bike into a car wash can hardly be said to be of sound mind, now, can he? [6]

Our bowls champion, (*name*), gives cause for a little dis-quiet also. His wife said to me only the other day, 'How can a man who's a bowls champion still manage to kick over all the milk bottles on the doorstep?'

And I hear that our boxing champion (*name*), has let his success go to his head. His wife tells me that ever since he won the cup he refuses to get up before the stroke of ten.

And what about our golf champion, (*name*)? I ask you, two weeks ago he woke up and found a burglar in the house, so what did he do? Crowned the intruder with a five iron. What a stupid thing to do – everyone knows the shot calls for an eight.

Our bridge champ doesn't inspire me with all that much confidence, either. After one game, I was kibbitzing, and he said to me, 'How do you think I should have played that last hand?' I said, 'Under an assumed name.'

(*Name*), our chess wizard, tells me that he practises with

his dog. Yes, his dog plays chess. I said to him, 'your dog must be very clever.' He said, 'Oh, I don't know, I can usually beat him three times out of four.'

Our cricket team didn't exactly shine this season, either. I was in the Pavilion one afternoon when the phone rang. I answered and it was a call for (*name of notoriously bad batsman*). So I said, 'Well, he's just going in to bat.' And the caller said, 'oh, all right, I'll hang on.'

I'm thinking of taking more interest in the swimming section of the club, though. Those bikinis are getting briefer and briefer, and then there's the kiss-of-life practice if anyone needs it. Mind you, if (*name of heavily bearded member*) gets into difficulties he can just drown.

We've had our usual crop of club marriages during the year, which should ensure a future generation of new members. Mind you, just because a chap gets married, it doesn't mean he should break training. I heard of one husband who was determined to keep in shape during his honeymoon, so there he was doing his press-ups one night on the floor of the bedroom in the honeymoon hotel. Up, down, up down, up down – eventually his bride said to him, 'Why don't you get into bed and kill two birds with one stone?'

There is one sport I haven't mentioned, so for the benefit of those ladies on the Pill the time is now eight-fifteen.[7]

Our cabaret tonight is something very special – songs from the soprano extraordinary. Mr. George Shorthouse (*or name of suitable member*); he was going to sing 'In A Monastery Garden' but he couldn't get over the wall, so instead he will oblige with 'You Stole My Gal, You Horse Thief, You.'

Here now then, to start us off with the waltz from King Kong are (*local band*).[8]

Suggested Headings

And in conclusion. Get this over/drinks free.
Good year. Membership drive. Good turn-out. TV must be lousy.

Hands up.

(*name*) looking smart. 'Got this suit backing a horse.'

Registration number gag.

Dream about (*name*). 'Thank goodness you've come. We're playing hell tomorrow!'

Finances not in good shape, unlike (*name*).

Raffle (*name's*) new set of clubs.

(*name*) can't be here. Refused bail.

(*name*) girl on R hand and girl on L hand. 'Gangrene'.

Told committee they were a set of addle-pated, boring, incompetent nincompoops, so they made him a Life Member.

Mens sana in corpore sano (Yiddish and gum arabic).

Sound mind in a sound body. Ideal the club strives for.

Football team. Ref elected man of the match.

Tennis. (*name*) drove motor bike into car wash.

Bowls. (*Name's*) wife said 'Bowls champion? Kicks over milk bottles.'

Boxing. Success has gone to (*name's*) head. Won't get up before stroke of 10.

Golf. (*name*) hit burglar with 5 iron. Stupid – should have been 8.

Bridge. 'How should I have played that last hand?' 'Under an assumed name.'

Chess. (*name*) practises with dog. 'Clever?' 'No, I beat him 3 times out of 4.'

Cricket. Phone call for (*name*) 'All right, I'll hang on.'

Swimming. Bikinis getting briefer and kiss-of-life practice. If (*name*) gets into difficulties he can drown.

Club marriages. One husband doing press-ups on honeymoon. 'Why not get into bed and kill two birds with one stone?'

Ladies on Pill time is now.

Cabaret. Soprano extraordinary, Mr. George Shorthouse. 'In A Monastery Garden' but couldn't get over the wall. 'You stole My Gal, You Horse Thief, You.'

Band. Waltz from King Kong.

Notes

Careful thought will need to be given to the personalities you mention, since both their sporting and personal characteristics will need to be general knowledge. If you feel that anyone will be offended by being left out, by all means mention them but without any qualifying joke. Don't let this list of anti-achievements go on for too long: the law of diminishing returns needs to be kept firmly in mind. Juvenal is pronounced *Joo*ven'l.

1. This is one occasion when you can laugh at your own joke. Don't forget to tell or sign to your audience to put their hands down. You will be surprised how many hands will remain in the air, and if people have gone along with your joke it is discourteous not to let them off the hook.

2. The name you choose should be a very well-known and long-established champion at his particular sport.

3. Here you will refer to a member who is renowned for being very pleased and proud of a new possession, or one whose ancient tennis-racket or snooker cue or whatever have been the butt of jokes for some time past.

4. This will be the Mayor or officer of a neighbouring club.

5. Pronounced 'mens *sar*-nar in *cor*por-ay *sar*-no'.

6. It doesn't have to be tennis, of course; this gag is best applied to a cup-winner who does in fact ride a motor bike.

7. Look at your watch when you give the time.

8. Give the band the cue to start at this point.

The following may be of possible use:

Our hand-picked team of experienced waitresses will bend over backwards to serve you . . . the snacks are all to be recommended – I understand that some of the sausages have been modelled from the life . . .

5

Armed Forces

Thank you. Good evening, ladies and gentlemen – that's the only part of my speech I've practised. From here on it's all nerve . . . crikey! [1] there's more brass here than in the regimental band . . . I am happy to tell you that I once had the pleasure of wearing Her Majesty's uniform for two years . . . of course, it fitted her better . . . [2]

I remember my medical so well; the MO said, 'Right – drop 'em!' So I put my cases down . . . and he said, 'Now, take your clothes off.' So I took my clothes off. He went outside to have a laugh . . . then he came back and said, 'Now, madam . . .' (*pause to look affronted*) well, it was cold. Then he said, 'You see that glass jar over there on the shelf? I want you to fill it.' I said, 'What – from here?'

He passed me, but the dentist wasn't keen. He said, 'I can't let you into the Army with those teeth!' I said, 'Well, you let my brother in with 'em last week!'

Then of course I had to have an Army haircut – but it's all healed up now. Then I went to the Quartermaster's stores to get my uniform. The sergeant said, 'How's the trousers, all right?' I said, 'Yes, fine, thank you, sergeant.' He said, 'What about the jacket?' I said, 'That seems a good fit, too, sergeant.' He said, 'Blimey – you must be deformed!'

But I enjoyed my time in Aldershot. I know I enjoyed Aldershot – it said so on page 34 of my orders. We all had a good time there – the CO's daughter was known as Apple, 'cos she was good to the corps.

But I come from an old military family. One of my ancestors fell at Waterloo . . . someone pushed him off platform five.[3] My great-grandfather was a soldier, too. He emigrated to America and joined the cavalry. He was at Custer's Last Stand. That was a very sad occasion – especially for Mrs. Custer.

Then there was my other great-grandfather – what a great fighter he was. He fought with Gordon at Khartoum, with Baden Powell and Redvers Buller in South Africa, and he fought with Kitchener and Haig . . . he couldn't get on with anybody. My grandfather was posted to France in the First World War. I asked him once what it was like. He said, 'I dunno, I never got out of the envelope.'[4]

Then during the Second World War I had an uncle who served with the Post Office Rifles, until he was unfortunately cashiered for some untoward dealings with the mails . . . that reminds me of my youth . . . I think he joined the Navy. Anyway . . .

My father had a good war. He was a captain – he achieved this exalted rank the hard way. He started as a colonel . . . but for a time he was ADC to Monty – ADC, that's Ada Camp – and he worshipped Monty. Worshipped the ground he walked on.

He told me once, when they were in North Africa, he was with Monty when a despatch rider came up with a message to say that five Panzer divisions were approaching the rear. Monty just turned to my old man and said, '(*Name*)' – that's the same as mine, you'll be surprised to learn – '(*name*), fetch me my wed tunic.' So Dad fetched Monty his red tunic, Monty put it on, issued his orders and the enemy were routed.

A few days later, the same thing happened: a despatch rider came up with news of ten Panzer divisions approaching dead ahead. And again Monty told my father to fetch his red tunic; he put it on, issued his orders and again the enemy were annihilated.

The following day, reports came of fifteen Panzer divisions approaching the right flank – again Monty put on his red tunic before doing battle; and on the day after that, when he heard that twenty Panzer divisions were approaching the left flank, yet again he sent for his red tunic before issuing the instructions which led to total defeat of the enemy.

My old man was a keen young officer – bit of a crawler, truth be known – so he plucked up the courage to ask the great general why, before going into battle, he always put his red tunic on.

'It's quite simple, my boy,' said Monty, 'it's camouflage. If I am wounded, and the twoops see that I'm hurt, they may lose the will to win; it might be fatal to mowale if I were seen to be injured, so I put on my wed tunic in order to disguise the bleeding, should it happen.'

Just then four despatch riders arrived at HQ with news that five thousand Panzer divisions were approaching the rear, ten Panzer divisions were approaching dead ahead, fifteen on the right flank and twenty on the left flank – simultaneously. Without batting an eyelid, Monty turned to my father and said, '(*name*), fetch me my bwown twousers...' [5]

But I'm the last of the line – apart from a sister in the Tank Corps . . . or was it the Medical Corps? Yes, it was the Medical Corps. Only she got chucked out – she treated an insane duck for piles...

You know, what I like about the Army is ... er ... it's ... er ... the ... er ... A funny thing happened to me when I got here. The sentry at the gate said 'Halt – who goes there?' I said, 'Oh, you wouldn't know me, I'm a visitor.' He said, 'Do you want the officers' mess?' I said, 'I didn't know he was married . . .' Just then the Chaplain arrived at the gate, and the sentry said, 'Halt – who goes there?' The padre said, 'Chaplain,' and the sentry said, 'Pass, Charlie.'

But it really is a great privilege for me to be here amongst you representatives of today's Armed Services, and when I look at you all, I know that I did not fight in vain. Thank you.

Suggested Headings

Only part practised – all nerve.
More brass than regimental band.
Wore HM's uniform for two years.
Medical. 'Drop 'em.' Cases down. Clothes off. Went for laugh.

'Now then, madam'. It was cold. Glass jar. 'What, from here?'

Haircut healed up now.

Uniform. Trousers fit, jacket fits. 'Deformed!'

Enjoyed Aldershot.

CO's daughter known as Apple.

Ancester fell at Waterloo.

Great-grandfather at Custer's Last Stand.

Other great-grandfather. Great fighter. Fought with Gordon at Khartoum, with Redvers Buller and Baden Powell in SA, with Kitchener and Haig.

Grandfather posted to France.

World War Two uncle in PO Rifles. Cashiered.

Reminds me of my youth. Joined Navy.

Father made captain the hard way.

ADC to Monty.

Red tunic – brown trousers.

Last of line except sister in Tank Corps.

No, Medical Corps. Insane duck.

What I like about the Army is.

Sentry. You wouldn't know me. Officers' mess.

Chaplain. 'Pass, Charlie'.

Privilege to be here. When I see you all, I know I did not fight in vain.

Notes

This speech is of course heavily Army-orientated, but most of the gags can readily be altered to suit the other two Services. Of course, many of the jokes will need considerable alteration if you are in uniform yourself, but then if you are a serving man you won't need me to tell you where the changes should be made. To the civilian contemplating addressing members of the Armed Forces I would offer a warning: be very careful not to offend. Serving men are extremely touchy about their regiments, corps, units, and traditions of their Service generally. They take their uniforms and all that goes with them very seriously indeed, and you must be on rock-solid ground to take the mickey out of a group of men whose loyalty to one another and to their group is the backbone of their lives. The Royal Navy would not appreciate being reminded of Churchill's famous dictum about 'Rum, sodomy and the lash'; the Army won't laugh at any mention of recent trouble spots – remember they sometimes get killed in action; the Royal Air Force are less encrusted with the barnacles of tradition but are still faithful to the memories of their heroes like Tedder, Trenchard and Harris.

Remember also that men in the Services tend to be very conservative in outlook and in political opinion, as indeed are all uniformed occupations like the police force, the fire service and so on. Anti-socialist references are therefore a sure bet, as are knocks against unions, bureaucracy, and permissiveness. On this last point, by the way, the old double-standard applies : if ladies are present, keep it clean, if they are not you can be as blue as you like (unless there is a very high-ranking officer present who, like the Queen at the Royal Variety Shows, will represent a sort of laughter-quotient catalyst).

If your audience is composed of members of the RAF, you might say, 'I have not flown much myself, it's much too frightening. The last civil airliner I flew in had an outside loo . . .' The fact that you find flying frightening will make them feel comfortingly superior to you, and then you follow this up with a laugh. Similarly, a Navy audience can be told : 'I'm always a nervous sailor –' (don't say you are a bad sailor, since many sailors are too – Nelson notoriously so). 'Once I had to go to the States, and half way across one of the officers – he could see I was scared to death – he said, "Don't worry, sir, we're only three miles from land." I said, "Only three miles from land? In the middle of the Atlantic?" He said, "Yes, straight down!"'

1. Use your own ejaculation if 'Crikey!' doesn't suit you.
2. Don't pause too long after 'for two years' or they'll be ahead of you.
3. Similarly don't wait too long after 'fell at Waterloo'.
4. This is only a quick quip and isn't worth waiting for,

except that you might alter the posting from France to any location recently visited by the troops you are addressing.

5. This is a very strong gag, unless you feel your audience might know it too well, or if you can't do the Monty voice. It doesn't have to be Monty, of course: I originally used to tell this gag about Gordon of Khartoum. It needs practising – the first paragraph to be taken quite slowly, the second a little faster. The third can be quite fast, since you are just taking your audience through narrative which they can foresee. The fourth paragraph again to be taken slowly and the fifth very fast, right up to the final sentence, which can be taken as slowly as you like.

If you feel the ladies present might object to the tag-line, I have included an alternative joke below.

• It is useful to remember that rivalry between outfits in the Services is just as strong as loyalty within them, and that one can easily be set against another.

Actually, I had a pal who was in the Royal Herbert recently (*alter to suit service and locality – the Royal Herbert Hospital is an Army hospital in Kent.*) Nothing serious – he's in the (*rival outfit*) and was suffering from boot-licker's tongue – and he told me that Her Majesty the Queen paid an official visit to the hospital. She went along the wards, and there, lying in one of the beds smartly at attention, was this old sweat from the Chelsea Pensioners. The Queen stopped by his bed and said, 'And how are you?'

He said, (*querulous old man voice*) 'I'm fine, thank you, Your Majesty. Very gracious of you to ask, Your Majesty.'

Then the Queen said, 'And why are you here?' The old chap replied, 'I got boils on me botty, Your Majesty!'

Well, of course, the CO and the matron and the staff were all furious – he'd put a blight on the whole occasion. So, after the Queen had gone they all came running in to the old boy's bedside and said, 'How dare you talk to the Queen like that! You've disgraced the whole hospital!'

The old chap said, 'Well, Her Majesty was kind enough to ask me what was wrong wi' me so I told 'er. What's wrong wi' that?'

The matron said, 'Well, you could have just said you were covered in boils and let it go at that. You didn't have to be so specific.'

Now, it so happened that a couple of weeks later the Prince of Wales also paid a visit to the same hospital, and by a remarkable coincidence . . . (*pause to allow to savour what is to come*) . . . he toured the same ward and stopped by the same bed, in which was lying the same old chap – at attention, thumbs down the seams of his sheets.

'And how are you?' asked the Prince.

'I'm very well, Your Royal 'Ighness, Very gracious of you to ask, Your Royal 'Ighness.'

'And what is your trouble?' asked the Prince.

The old boy looked round, and there were the CO, the doctors, the matron and all the top brass, glaring at him, so he said, 'Er, well, Your Royal 'Ighness – I'm, er, covered in boils!'

'I see,' said the Prince. 'So they've spread since my Mother was here!'

This gag gives plenty of scope for acting. Use any accent which is comfortable for the old soldier and differentiate the voices sharply, but don't parody the Queen – this won't go down all that well with a Services audience. 'By a remarkable coincidence' is a nice booster laugh, and you can also insert 'D'you like the accent?' somewhere in one of the old sweat's speeches. Keep the story line moving along so that it doesn't get tedious, and take the tag line slowly: I'll be surprised if you don't get a round of applause.

6

Birthday Party: Proposal

Brethren and sisteren – we are gathered here today . . . you have all come to be saved, haven't you . . . to do honour unto our brother (*name*), and to help in celebrating his birthday. Or at least in drinking his beer . . . he is now approaching thirty . . . (*pause for reaction*) . . . I didn't say from which direction . . . but if the Biblical maximum is three score years and ten, then (*name*) is definitely on the way out.[1]

Now (*name*) is the salt of the earth – a bit gritty at times – but he's a chap we are all fond of . . . some of us very fond – aren't we, Cynthia? [2] – which is why we are all here. He is a fine, upstanding figure of a man – isn't he, (*name of wife*) [3] . . . ? (*as though she has just said something*): Once a fortnight? . . . oh, well, it comes to us all . . . He is handsome, honest, charming, sober – sober? – industrious, kind, intellig – who wrote this rubbish? [4]

Anyway, he comes, as many of you know, from (*place of origin*) – and they were glad to see him go – no! – where at school he distinguished himself by getting the School Cert at the early age of fourteen . . . she was a saucy little blonde number, I believe . . . [5]

He then spent two years in the Armed Forces, rising to the rank of Private, Third Class, smoking . . . [6] on returning to civvy street he tried to get a job as a sex maniac, but he failed the medical. Then he became a Corporation dustman – £5 a week and as much as he could eat. That's when we first met, as a matter of fact. It was just before Christmas and he banged on my door. I opened it, (*name*) was standing there and I said, 'Yes?' He said, 'I'm your dustman.' I said, 'Oh yes?' He said, 'Well, it's Christmas.' I said, 'So what?' He said, 'I'm the chap who empties your dustbins.' I said, 'Well, I'm the chap who fills 'em up – push off!'[7] . . . Do you remember that, (*name*)? I'll never forget it – oh, the language!

Still, we became good friends after I got out of hospital, and today we see him, a valued (*give the subject's job*), a pillar of society . . . well, if not a pillar at least a flying buttress – he's always leaning on somebody – a devoted husband to (*name of wife*) and father to (*names of the children, if any*),[8] whom we are all proud to know. So to you, (*name*), with our love – Happy Birthday!

Suggested Headings

Brethren and sisteren – gathered – saved.
Celebrating – drinking his beer.
Approaching thirty.
Biblical maximum.
Salt of the earth.
All fond of him – Cynthia.
Fine upstanding figure.
Once a fortnight.
Handsome, honest, charming, sober, industrious, kind, intellig –
Comes from (*place of origin*).
At school – School Cert.
Two years in Armed Forces. Pte 3rd class smoking.
Sex maniac.
Corporation dustman. £5 a week. Christmas.
Good friends after I got out of hospital.
Valued (*occupation*).
Pillar of society – flying buttress.
Devoted husband to (*name of wife*).
Father to (*names of children*).
All proud to know.

Notes

This is obviously a short speech – at a party nobody will thank you for a formal disquisition. Obviously you will concentrate on the subject's life history and life style; his

58

hobbies and occupation might be mentioned, and certainly his family. Note the little touch of sentiment at the close – this is very important. His physical appearance can be utilised – height, weight, clean-shaven or not, etc., etc., for instance –

If bald:

> He's the only man I know who combes his hair with a sponge. Would you mind moving back a bit? The light from your head is shining in my eyes.
>
> I remember him when he had a beautiful crop of golden curls. That was before he joined the (*firm*), or before he started playing golf.

If bearded:

> That face fungus of his has tickled the ladies' fancies in six countries to my certain knowledge.
>
> See West Indian barber gag on page 25.

If tall:

> He's 6ft 6in in his stocking feet. He wears tall stockings.

If fat:

> (*Name*), it's said that inside every fat man there's a thin one trying to get out. Well, you just keep him where he is because we like you just as you are.

If short:

> It is said that good things come in little packages. I don't know who said it but whoever it was obviously had never met (*name*).

The speech suggested above is written for a man's birthday; for a woman much of the patter can be easily altered, but I would warn you against being too personal or rude. Men are used to being insulted, in fact on an occasion such as this it is expected, but women are not, so go carefully. After the detailed notes I have appended some extra gags for use on a lady's birthday which you will notice are largely angled against the husband or boy-friend, which is the safest course to follow.

59

1. 'Approaching thirty' – always choose the decade *below* the actual age; obviously the 'Biblical maximum' gag will be omitted if the subject's age is below thirty-five or so. Don't use this gag for a woman!
2. The girl's name here should refer to a new girl friend, or perhaps to a younger sister of the subject's wife.
3. If there is no wife this will be a reference to the current girl friend.
4. Give some air between each of the complimentary adjectives, to allow time for ironical cheering.
5. The School Certificate was replaced by the General Certificate of Education in 1952, so this gag cannot strictly apply to anyone born after about 1936. If the subject is too young for this gag, therefore, you might say: 'He was the headmaster's pet – they kept him in a cage'.
6. Similarly, National Service was abolished in 1960 so this joke will not apply (unless of course the subject has been a volunteer) to anyone born after about 1942. Alternatively you could say, 'After school he didn't get a job for some time. He just lay around the house all day long, playing his guitar and singing work songs'.
7. 'Push off!' can be made stronger according to the company.
8. If the subject is not married, say 'A dedicated bachelor – sorry about that Cynthia...'

Gags for Lady's Birthday

Actually, I met the (*name of subject's husband or boyfriend*) in the Dog and Duck last week – I'd gone in to change my breath – and he said, 'It's (*name*)'s birthday next week.' 'Really?' I said. 'What are you getting for her?' He said, 'What are you offering.'

I said to her, 'What do you want for your birthday?' She said, 'An alligator bag'. I said, 'Why do you want to carry an alligator round with you?'

I remember her last birthday. I said, 'How old are you

now then?' She said, 'I've just reached twenty-nine.' I said, 'What kept you?'

Her husband's given her a wonderful present this year – a mink outfit. I kid you not, it's a mink outfit. Two steel traps and a gun.

She's always been a beauty. When she was eighteen she had her picture done in oils. She dropped her photograph in the chip pan.

7

Birthday Party: Reply

(*After 'Happy Birthday To You' has been sung*) That's the first time I've been serenaded by forty drunks at the same time. (*To proposer*) thank you, Fatty [1] – who invited him . . . ? – thank you for those few ill-chosen words . . . And I'd like to thank again those of you who bought me presents. And for those who didn't the bar is now closed!

But sincerely, it's so great to be surrounded by one's friends – those kind and wonderful friends who'd do anything for a pal . . . even the washing-up!

I did have some entertainment lined up for you, but Liza Minelli couldn't make it.[2] Charlie Screech threatened to sing for us, but I gave him another scotch so that took care of that.[3] Harry Sludge said he'd give us a selection from Top of the Slops on the bass tuba, but he's feeling rather puckered out – what have you been doing to him, Jane.[4] Ivor Cough said he'd tell us some fairy stories, but he feels the vibes aren't right.[5] Lydia Dustbin promised to do a strip, but someone's pinched her fan.[6] And Arthur Mometer said he'd tell us some jokes, but he's lost his matchboxes [7] . . . so you'll just have to make do with my records.

And once again, I do thank you all so very much for making my birthday such a happy and . . . drunken one. Thank you.

Suggested Headings

Serenaded by forty drunks.
Fatty – who invited him?
Thanks for presents – bar closed.
Surrounded by friends – washing up.
Entertainment.
    Charlie Screech to sing – give him scotch.

Harry Sludge: selection from Top of the Slops on bass tuba.

Puckered out.

Ivor Cough: fairy stories but vibes aren't right.

Lydia Dustbin: strip but fan pinched.

Arthur Mometer: tell jokes about lost matchboxes.

Again thanks for happy and drunken birthday.

Notes

This speech is so short that you might attempt it without notes, although I would still make the headings and practise from them. The reaction to a speech of this kind is always enthusiastically rowdy; everyone is full of goodwill and alcohol, so you needn't worry about it falling flat, for whatever you say will be greeted with delight – and probably cheers and applause.

The text may seem rather short, and certainly the time it takes to deliver will depend largely on how many of your friends you fit into the 'entertainment' section, but since everything you say will almost certainly be greeted with heckling and witty(?) interjections, you may well find that you'll be on your feet for a lot longer than you expect.

But don't let it get out of hand. Once you feel the interest dropping, perhaps because your guests are getting a touch overexcited, cut to the final thank-you bit.

1. If your proposer is in fact fat, refer to him as 'Tiny'; if he is tall, call him 'Shorty', if bald 'Curly', if short 'Lofty' and so on. But don't be too cruel – 'Creep', 'git' or 'berk' are just insulting without any particular humorous connotations.
2. Or 'Bay City Rollers' or whoever is the latest rave. Or you can go to the other extreme and say 'Des O'Connor (or Ruby Murray) couldn't make it.'
3. 'Charlie Screech' will be one of your guests famed for his appalling singing – or he could be someone with a good voice who *always* sings at parties, at great length.
4. 'Harry Sludge' could be a brass or wind-playing friend,

or he could be just someone a touch eccentric or way out. 'Jane' will be his wife or girlfriend.

5. 'Ivor Cough' can be (a) a gay friend (male), although this is fraught with dangers and should only be used if you are absolutely sure that neither he nor your other guests is going to be disturbed by the reference;
(b) an extremely butch (again male!) friend renowned for his manly pursuits such as rugby, beer, sports cars and women.

6. 'Lydia Dustbin' will be the Belle of the Ball.

7. 'Arthur Mometer' will of course be the local storyteller; if he is also a bit of a bore, as inveterate joke-tellers so often are, this quip will go down all the better. Nor should it offend any poor man's Bob Hope.

An alternative opening: after 'those ill-chosen words', if you think the assembly will appreciate the reference, you can say: 'That speech sounded like the opening plea for Dreyfus.'

8

Christening: Proposal

A baby has been defined as an alimentary canal with a loud voice at one end and no sense of responsibility at the other . . . The last christening I went to they named the boy after his father – they called him Dad . . . I'm an only child my-self.[1] When I was born my parents took one look at me and decided they couldn't possibly improve on nature . . . Actually, the day I was born my father gave everyone a cigar. Mine was a little strong but I finished it . . . At first I was called 6⅞ths – my father picked the name out of a hat . . . We were very poor, though – even my mother was on HP.

I'm not really an only child. In actual fact – I do have a younger brother. I was so disappointed when he was born; still, at least it stopped me teasing the cat.

I asked Lucy[2] what her new brother's name was and she said, 'I dunno – he can't talk yet,' I said. 'I suppose he's a lovely pink colour?' And she said, 'no – he's an 'orrible yeller!'

Actually, my next-door neighbours have seventeen children . . . seventeen – they must be stork raving mad . . . I remember I once said to the woman next door, 'Why so many?' And she said, 'Well, I'm a bit hard of hearing.' I said, 'What's that got to do with it?' She said, 'Well, when my old man and me go off to bed, he always says to me, 'Well – are we going to have a cup of cocoa or what?' And I say – 'What?''

She's called Liza, by the way, and her husband's name is Ferdy. They called their youngest Ferdiliser . . . well, what do you expect at this time of day – wit? . . . There are some funny names about nowadays, though, aren't there? I heard of a baby the other day called Glug-Glug – the vicar fell in the font . . . But I went to a christening once, and as I handed the baby to the vicar he said to me, 'And what's this little chap's name?' I said. 'No, it's a girl, vicar – you've got hold of my thumb.'

So, anyway, we come to today's centre of attractions, the cynosure of all eyes: James.[3] I know that the choice of his name caused a few pursed lips and raised eyebrows in the family. One of his great-aunts was very disappointed when Freda [4] told her. 'Oh, Freda,' she said, 'you can't call him James. Every Tom, Dick and Harry's called James...'

Mind you, they had thought of calling him John Nebuchadnezzer Ethelred Montmorency Jones,[5] but I talked them out of that. 'Look,' I said, 'you can't call the poor little lad "John"...' so, James it is, and with such a mother I am sure he'll grow in grace and charm and intelligence,[6] and with such a father I am sure he'll ... er ... he'll ... er ... ah, well, nobody's perfect. After all, never forget that the person who has everything will soon find himself in quarantine.

Congratulations, then, Freda – we all knew you had it in you ... and as for you, Harry,[7] standing there looking all smug and sleek in your interview suit – I can smell the mothballs from here – looking as though butter wouldn't melt in your pipe ... He's all cool, calm and collected now but I was told that when he got news of the baby's arrival instead of asking 'Boy or girl?' he said, 'Am I a father or a mother?'

Seriously, this child has been born into a hard, hard world, but we can be sure that in the family in which he is lucky enough to find himself he will receive the maximum amount of love and the best possible start in life. So, well done, Harry; well done, Freda; and young James – here's to you! [8]

Suggested Headings

Alimentary canal. Loud voice/sense of responsibility.
Boy named after father – Dad.
I'm only child. Parents couldn't possibly improve on nature.

Day of birth father gave everyone a cigar.

$6\frac{7}{8}$ths.

Very poor. Mother on HP.

Not only child. Stopped me teasing the cat.

Asked Lucy brother's name.

Lovely pink colour?

Next-door neighbours have 17 children. Stork raving mad.

Hard of hearing. Cup of cocoa or what?

Liza-Ferdy. Ferdiliser.

Glug-glug.

What's little chap's name? Thumb.

Cynosure of all eyes: James.

Great-aunt: Tom, Dick and Harry.

John Nebuchadnezzar Ethelred Montmorency Jones.

With such a mother grace/charm/intelligence.

Quarantine.

Congrats, Freda. Knew you had it in you.

Harry 'father or mother?'

Seriously . . .

Notes

1. If it is well-known to your audience that you are not in fact an only child then obviously this gag should be omitted. If you are the youngest of the family then the gag can be altered to suit, i.e. 'I'm the youngest in our family. When I was born etc., etc.'.
2. Lucy is the new baby's elder brother or sister. If it is a first child perhaps a young cousin's name can be used.
3. Obviously the name must be changed to suit; also the sex if necessary.
4. Freda: the mother.
5. Jones: the surname of the new arrival.
6. If you are referring to a girl, add beauty.
7. Harry: the father.
8. If alcohol is available this should be expanded to the customary: 'I ask you all to charge your glasses and to drink to the health and happiness of this most welcome newcomer:

Here's to the happiest days of your life,
Spent in the arms of another man's wife – your mother!
To James!'

The following gags are useful in the event of twins (or even triplets):

I saw Murphy rushing up the street yesterday in a terrible state. 'What's up?' I asked him.

'Bridget's just had twins!' he roared at me furiously. 'Just wait till I lay hands on the other fella!'

The twins were being admired in the park by a sweet old lady. She peered into the pram for a few minutes, then straightened up and said to the mother decisively, 'I should keep the one on the left.'

Two pals, one a recent father·and the other about to become one, were talking.

'It's a funny thing,' said the new daddy, 'but while my wife was expecting Jack and Jill she was reading a book called "Heavenly Twins".'

'Blimey, don't say that!' exclaimed the other. 'My wife's reading "Birth of a Nation"!'

What an achievement – in my family childlessness is hereditary . . .

These gags should be heavily personalized; even when your listeners know you are only telling a joke they will find it three times as funny if the characters and events in the story, however far-fetched, are connected to people they know – and especially to the parents, grandparents, and siblings of the new infant.

Monday's child is fair of face,
Tuesday's child is full of grace;
Wednesday's child is full of woe,
Thursday's child has far to go.
Friday's child is loving and giving,
Saturday's child works hard for its living.
And a child that is born on the Sabbath day,
Is fair and wise and good and gay.

*　　　　*　　　　*

68

The following may be told if it is apparent that no maiden aunties are likely to take offence:

Did you hear about the three babies who were talking things over? They were discussing their feeds, and one said, 'I'm on Cow and Gate. It's very good for me – very nutritious.'

The second baby said, 'Well, I'm on Benger's. That's very good for me, too, and it tastes delicious.'

The third baby said, 'I'm on natural feed. Natural – mother's milk.'

'Oh, are you?' said the other two. 'What's it like, then?'

'Oh, it's great,' said the infant. 'The only trouble is I have to share it with a chap who smokes St. Bruno . . .'

An explorer who came home after a year's absence was distraught to find a new-born baby nestling in his wife's arms. He rushed to the doctor for an explanation.

'Don't worry about it,' said the doctor. 'That's what we in the profession call a grudge baby.'

'A grudge baby?'

'Yes – someone's had it in for you.'

Freda's a game kid, though. James was a bit troublesome about making his arrival, so the doctor picked up one of those fearsome-looking steel instruments.

'Don't worry,' he said to her. 'I'm not going to hurt you.'

As he pulled up her nightie she grabbed him between the legs and said, 'Now we're not going to hurt each other, are we . . . ?'

Signs of the Zodiac

Aries, the Ram	March 21–April 19
Taurus, the Bull	April 20–May 20
Gemini, the Twins	May 21–June 21
Cancer, the Crab	June 22–July 22
Leo, the Lion	July 23–Aug. 22
Virgo, the Virgin	Aug. 23–Sept. 22
Libra, the Balance	Sept. 23–Oct. 23
Scorpio, the Scorpion	Oct. 24–Nov. 21
Saggitarius, the Archer	Nov. 22–Dec. 21

Capricorn, the Goat	Dec. 22–Jan. 19
Aquarius, the Water-Carrier	Jan. 20–Feb. 18
Pisces, the Fishes	Feb. 19–March 20

Birthstones

Modern trade alternatives are given in brackets

January	Garnet
February	Amethyst
March	Bloodstone (Aquamarine)
April	Diamond (White sapphire)
May	Emerald
June	Pearl (Alexandrite)
July	Ruby
August	Sardonyx (Peridot)
September	Sapphire
October	Opal (Rozicron)
November	Topaz
December	Turquoise (Zircon)

Name Days

A glance at the notice board in any church porch will tell you what Feast Day or Saint's Day coincides with the natal day of the child being christened. Check in your diary also –special dates such as Guy Fawkes Day, Midsummer Day, Hallowe'en, Leap Year Day, etc., should be worked into your speech.

9

Christening: Reply

by the father of the new baby

I won't keep you long (*disclosing a thick wad of notes*) . . .
Thank you for those few unwelcome words [1] . . . Who wrote
your speech – Boris Karloff? [2] . . . No, as I said I won't
keep you long. The last time I made a speech Freda told
me I missed two very good opportunities. I said, 'What –
to tell a joke?' She said, 'No – to sit down.' So I'll keep it
brief.

Thank you so much for coming to pay your respects to
our precious little . . . (*yawn*) . . . angel . . . No, it is not
true that we are calling his pram a blunderbus . . . He is
very much a wanted baby, which is why we thought of calling him Onyx – short for Onyxpected . . . But it's wonderful having him in the house, with all those nappies festooned around. There are so many we've got a permanent
rainbow in the hall.

And as I know many of you ladies are interested in the
more basic details, I am happy to announce that James
weighed in at —lbs —oz, and that he now weighs —lbs
—oz. This splendid achievement is due entirely to Freda,
who is feeding him herself. This is of course the best way,
for five very good reasons – the feed is always the right
temperature, it is handy for picnics, it's ready mixed . . . it's
beautifully packaged . . . and the cat can't get at it.

Mind you, if I hadn't been on nights for so long we'd
have had this do a year ago . . . But we are very thrilled to
have produced this magnificent infant, who I am sure you
will all agree is just about the finest, most wonderful baby
of all time, the most . . . (*peers at notes, then says aside to
wife*) I can't read your writing, darling . . .

I think Freda's done a wonderful job, don't you? My –
er – contribution was made some time ago so I take no
credit for the final product. He's obviously intelligent – he

gets his brains from his mother's side, I think . . . yes, he must have – we've still got ours . . . and as for his looks! Well as the poet said 'Beauty is Truth, Truth Beauty', and as James is well and truly here he must be beautiful . . . (*look upwards with relief at having wangled tactfully out of an awkward corner*).

For all the marvellous gifts of toys and clothes and spoons and so on I'd like to thank you from the bottom of my cheque book. . . . Once again thank you very much for coming to honour our new son, and on his behalf may I end by saying: (*give a few seconds of baby gurglings and goo-gooing*). Thank you.

Suggested Headings

Unwelcome words – Boris Karloff.

Two very good opportunities.

Thank you for coming. Precious little (*yawn*) angel. Blunderbus.

Very much wanted. Onyx(pected).

Nappies festooned. Rainbow in hall.

Weight at birth.

Weight now.

Natural feed. Right temp, handy for picnics, ready mixed, beautifully packaged. Cat can't get at it.

If I hadn't been on nights.

Finest, most wonderful baby of all time (can't read).

Freda's done a splendid job – my contribution made some time ago.

Intelligent, brains from his mother's side, we've still got ours.

Looks. Beauty is Truth and Truth Beauty. Well and truly here so he must be beautiful.

Thanks for gifts from bottom of my cheque book.

Thanks for coming and may I say on his behalf: Goo-Goo!

Notes

1. Obviously, if the proposal has not been especially funny you will not say 'unwelcome'. Check with the proposer beforehand.
2. Boris Karloff. Names of personalities can lose impact and topicality very quickly so try to think of a name which is meaningful to your group – i.e. a theatrical group might appreciate the name Ibsen, a legal group Edgar Lustgarten, and so on.

10

Christmas Party

Christmas is coming, the geese are getting fat;
Please put a penny in the old man's hat.
If you haven't got a penny, a ha'penny will do;
If you haven't got a penny – you must be Harry Sludge! [1]

Well, now – are you having a good time? . . . I'll soon put a stop to that . . . Stand by for more poetry – Christmas comes but once a year, and when it comes it brings good cheer . . . pass the bicarb, someone . . . what a spread, eh? No, I'm not talking about Brenda's waistline [2] I'm talking about all this lovely grub. What about a cheer for poor Mum who's spent all morning slaving over a hot sofa . . . (*cheers*) and one for Dad who's paid for it . . . (*more cheers*) and for young Alf here who's spent all day slaving over a hot telly . . . [3]

Dad had a hard time stuffing the turkey, though. If he'd stuffed it any more he'd have damn near killed it . . . But it's wonderful to spend Christmas surrounded by friends and loved ones . . . last year we had my mother-in-law for Christmas lunch [4] . . . but I'm glad we're back to turkey again this year . . . I got that one out of last year's crackers . . .

And I'm happy to inform you that there's not only plenty of food but plenty to drink as well – not that Dennis needs telling.[5] Hey, Dennis! – is that a drink or are you waiting to see the doctor . . . ? Yes, the booze will be flowing like glue. Now, Harry, you won't disgrace yourself again this year, will you? [6] Don't sit there looking the picture of innocence. Who was it fell off the roof in a drunken stupor, eh? I rushed out when I heard the bump and said, 'What happened?' Harry said, 'I dunno – I've only just got here myself.'

You can laugh, Dave . . . I heard about you, too . . . you

were the one who was walking home at one o'clock in the morning. As you went past the town hall you put a penny in a letter-box, looked up at the clock tower and said, 'Crikey, I've lost half a stone!'[7] We'll be playing your favourite game again this year, Dave. You know, it's called Christmas Tree – you just stand in the corner and get lit up.

Mind you, it happens all round. As Ben and I were coming in yesterday he looked across the street and said, 'I see the Browns are carrying in the Yule Log,' I said, 'don't be daft – that *is Brown* . . .'[8]

It has turned a bit chilly now, though, hasn't it? I must get Granny's legs lagged . . .

By the way, did you know Johnny was born on December 24th . . .[9] He told me he wanted to be home for Christmas . . . But I always get sentimental at this time of year . . . aaaaah . . . yes, every Christmas Eve I take off my socks and stand them in front of the fire . . .

One of the things to look forward to during the festive season is the good old pantomime . . . the last one I saw was a Jewish pantomime, actually – 'Abe's In The Wood' . . . then there's 'Robinson Beanstalk!' . . . and of course there's Gloria's favourite: 'Dick In The Woods' . . .[10]

I hope Father Christmas brought you all nice presents. Of course, I believe in Father Christmas, don't you? Oh, yes, I do – Father Christmas is definitely not a myth . . . he's a mythter . . . They don't write jokes like that any more . . . thank God . . . But some fathers are so mean – did you hear about one father who went out with a shotgun on Christmas Eve? He fired it into the air, came back in the house and told the kids he'd just shot Santa Claus . . . One day he came in and said, 'Now we can have a really Merry Christmas. I've just found a tree.' And he had, too – they lived in it for years . . . But did you hear about the Jewish Father Christmas? He came down the chimney and said, 'Hello, children. Merry Christmas – wanna buy some toys?'

But it's fun kissing the girls under the mistletoe, isn't it, Brian,[11] eh? . . . oh, you prefer kissing them under the nose, I see . . . Did you hear about the ugly girl? The boys hung her up and kissed the mistletoe [12] . . .

I've bought my mother-in-law a beautiful chair . . . I only hope the wife lets me plug it in . . . Grannie's got a new dressing-gown this year. Well, I noticed last year that no matter how cold it was she would go out and get the coal in her nightie. I said I'd get her a shovel but she said no, she wanted a dressing-gown . . . Rita's got a wonderful mink outfit – two steel traps and a gun. I hope Auntie Flo enjoys her crash-helmet – I'm not sure that cerise is quite your colour, Flo . . . Joy told me she doesn't want much – she'll settle for a five pound box of money . . . I'm sure Junior will derive hours of innocent pleasure from his home embalming kit – anyone seen the cat? I wanted to get George a present but I didn't know how to wrap up a pub . . . Glyn and Beryl have got a lovely diving suit (*look more closely at notes*) . . . no, sorry – divan suite . . .[13]

Well, now, I know you all want to get on with the party, and we're about to start dancing to Knuckles O'Reilly and his Ditch Diggers, so I'll finish now by saying;

> *Here's to you, as good as you are,*
> *Here's to me, as bad as I am,*
> *But as good as you are and as bad as I am,*
> *I'm as good as you are – as bad as I am.*
> *Merry Christmas!*

Suggested Headings

Christmas is coming etc: Harry Sludge.
Good time? Soon put a stop.
Christmas comes but once a year.
What a spread – Brenda's waistline. Lovely grub.
Mum slaving over a hot sofa.
Dad who's paid for it.
Alf slaving over hot telly.
Dad stuffed turkey – near killed it.
Last year ma-in-law for lunch.
Plenty to drink. Dennis.
Drink or are you waiting to see the doctor?
Booze flowing like glue.

Harry. Fell off the roof. What happened? Dunno – only just got here myself.

Dave. 1.00 a.m. by Town Hall. Penny in letter-box. Looks up at clock tower. Crikey. I've lost half a stone!

Favourite game. Christmas Tree. Stand in corner and get lit up.

Ben saw Browns carrying in Yule Log. That *is* Brown.

Chilly. Get Granny's legs lagged.

Johnny born Dec. 24th. Wanted to be home for Christmas.

Get sentimental. Take socks off every Christmas Eve and stand them in front of the fire.

Pantomime. Abe's In The Wood. Robinson Beanstalk, Gloria's favourite: Dick In The Woods.

Presents? Father Christmas definitely not a myth – a mythter.

Mean father. Shot Father Christmas. Found a tree. Family lived in it for years.

Jewish Father Christmas – wanna buy some toys.

Fun kissing girls under mistletoe. Brian prefers kissing them under the nose.

Ugly girl. Boys hung her up and kissed mistletoe.

List joke presents.

Knuckles O'Reilly & His Ditch Diggers

> *Here's to you, as good as you are,*
> *Here's to me, as bad as I am.*
> *But as good as you are and as bad as I am,*
> *I'm as good as you are – as bad as I am.*

Notes

1. Harry Sludge will, of course, be someone in the party renowned for 'closeness' – but be careful not to offend. You don't want to spoil someone's party for them, so pick on a character you are sure will appreciate the joke. This can be altered to 'If you haven't got a ha'penny – you must work for Sludge & Co' if the party is being given for employees of a particular firm. In other words – alter to suit.

2. Brenda can either be the ranking beauty in the gather-

ing, or a mum-to-be. Do not refer to someone who really is fat unless you are quite sure they will not mind.

3. This of course only makes sense if young Alf is famous for his addiction to television. Alter to suit.

4. If she is present or recently deceased you will naturally alter this to 'Last year we had old Jim Pules for Christmas lunch . . .'

5. Dennis will be a well-known elbow-lifter.

6. Harry will be another.

7. Dave also – if in London you can describe this event as taking place on Westminster Bridge with Big Ben as the clock tower.

8. The Browns can be neighbours.

9. Johnny is another guest chosen at random, the idea being to include as many people into your speech as possible. If the party is quite small try to give everyone a mention, and the more preposterous the story the bigger the laugh.

10. 'Dick In The Woods' Gloria will be the flighty girl of the party – but beware: don't use this gag if there is any possibility of her family being offended. After all, the implications of the joke are none too complimentary.

11. Brian will be the Lothario of the group.

12. Don't use this gag is there is only too evidently an ill-favoured girl in the party.

13. As I have said above, if the party is not too large try to invent a gag for everyone present. Other possibilities are given in the other speeches, as 'prizes', i.e. a week's free holiday on the Goodwin Sands; a 5lb tin of rat poison and a years' supply of rats; 'Gloria gets the privilege of escorting me home after the party,' etc. etc. etc.

11

Civic Function

Mr. Mayor, ladies and gentlemen, may I say first of all how thrilled I am to be here in (*name of local rival town*) ... what? ... oh, Sludgeville! I'm so sorry – I must have the wrong shirt on ... (*glance at cuff and rub off imaginary note*). Of course I know I'm in Sludgeville – who could mistake the smell – No! What I mean is, most sincerely, I like Sludgeville ... as a (w)hole ... well, you see, some years ago I spent a year here ... one Wednesday afternoon ...[1]

But in fact the reason I'm always so delighted to be here is that I used to have relations here. I won't say who with but it was a wonderful summer ... and in any case I always feel at home here. I feel that they are all my kind of people in Sludgeville – you know, skint ... but everyone is still so friendly. I wanted to send a postcard home so I popped into this little newsagent's in (*local*) street [2] ... that's a nice part of the world, isn't it? (*roll your eyes to heaven at the thought of the squalor*) ... Anyway, there was a lovely girl behind the counter, really beautiful – they all are here aren't they? ... (*looking around*) ... oh, I dunno, though ... but there was this very sweet creature smiling at me. She said, 'Yes?' I said, 'Wait a minute – I haven't asked you yet!' Well, I thought that was very friendly, don't you think? [3]

We are of course honoured tonight by the presence of the first citizen of Sludgeville and various civic dignitaries. I am sure you will never have the embarrassment such as befell the borough of Wantage – do you remember what happened there? ... no? well –

> *There was a young lady of Wantage,*
> *Of whom the Town Clerk took advantage!*
> *Said the Borough Surveyor,*

> *'You'll just have to pay 'er,*
> *You've considerably altered her frontage!'*

I'm sure there'll be nothing like that here . . .[4]

But what a marvellous Town Hall you have here. I said to the Mayor just before dinner, 'This is a superb building – what about the acoustics?' And he said, 'Well, I think they should be all right – the Mayoress and me have personally inspected all the toilets and we haven't noticed a smell in any of 'em . . .' And while on the subject, I must admit I was a bit saucy. I looked at that chain and said, 'What's that, then?' He said, 'That's my chain of office.' I said, 'If I pull it, do you flush?' He said, 'Every mayor of Sludgeville wears this during his year of office.' I said, 'Really? – where I come from we let him run around loose.'

But your mayor's as sharp as a tack when needs be. I heard he was canvassing one time and a chap said to him, 'I wouldn't vote for you if you were St. Peter himself.' To which he replied, 'If I was St. Peter you wouldn't be in my ward . . .'

Well, anyway, your grace . . . er, royal highness . . . er, warship . . . eh? worship [5] oh, all right . . . (*kneels down then realizes*) . . . oh! *worship!!!* yes, of course. You've been so kind to me it seems very ungracious to confess that I don't really like sitting down to dine with local councillors – well, they take so long to pass things. But I am sure, your worship, that you follow the two golden rules of holders of your ancient and noble office: you must suffer fools glady and answer your mail by return of post! Talking of letters, in local government I know you have to deal with a bewildering variety of problems – and that's almost as hard to say as to do – some of these letters will show you what I mean (*produce letters*):

> *Dear Sir, our ceiling has fallen down. Yours thankfully . . .*
>
> *Mrs. Smith next door has got no clothes. She hasn't had any for over a year now. The vicar has been visiting her regularly.*

I am glad to say that my husband who was reported missing is now dead.

In answer to yours I have given birth to a boy weight ten pounds. Is this satisfactory?

In reply to your kind enquiry I was married last week. I am sorry I made this error.

Will you be kind enough to send along the rat-catcher as my husband will be home Saturday afternoon.

That letter about owing rent reminds me that only this afternoon I found myself passing the local rent office so I thought I'd pop in to see what it was like. And there was this woman with a five pound note stuck in each ear! I said to one of the staff 'What's all that about, then?' He said, 'Oh, pay no attention. She's ten pounds in arrears . . .'

But seriously, your worships, ladies and gentlemen, it is quite genuinely and most sincerely a very great pleasure and privilege for me to be with you tonight and to renew my acquaintanceship [6] with the kind and friendly people of this delightful and historic – (*aside*) – what a creep . . .

Well, Somerset Maugham said that at a dinner one should eat wisely but not too well, and talk well but not too wisely. I am not sure which I've done tonight, so I'll sit down while you're still on my side. Thank you.

Suggested Headings

Wrong shirt.

Who could mistake the smell.

As a whole . . . spent a year here one Wednesday afternoon.

Relations.

To send postcard went into newsagent's in (*local*) street.

Yes? Haven't asked you yet.

> *There was a young lady of Wantage,*
> *Of whom the Town Clerk took advantage!*
> *Said the Borough Surveyor,*
> *'You'll just have to pay 'er,*
> *You've considerably altered her frontage!'*

Superb building – acoustics.

Chain – do you flush!

Where we come from we let him run around loose.

Wouldn't vote for you if you were St. Peter. If I were you wouldn't be in my ward.

Worship (kneel).

Councillors take so long to pass things.

Suffer fools gladly and answer your letters by return of post.

Joke letters in full.

£5 note in each ear. £10 in arrears.

Genuinely a great pleasure and privilege etc. (what a creep).

Somerset Maugham said 'eat wisely but not too well and talk well but not too wisely'.

Notes

1. The day should be the local half-day closing day.
2. The street should be a notoriously rough part of the town.
3. The last sentence is just to cover the pause between the tag-line and the laugh.
4. This sentence should be delivered to the Mayor or local dignitary, and also covers the gap between 'frontage' and the laugh. This is a sure-fire boffo. After this laugh you could add 'after all this isn't –' naming the local rival borough.
5. It can be a help to have a prompt planted at a table near you. If the kneeling is impractical, salam deeply instead.
6. If it is your first visit to the town alter to 'and to make the acquaintance of'.

A speech of this kind can easily be strengthened by saying, 'This town has special associations for me – I met my wife here' which then leads you into honeymoon jokes. Or if the town is itself a holiday town you can say you spent your honeymoon there – 'We had a quiet family wedding; just me, the wife and the kids'. If it is a seaside town there are the customary bathing jokes – 'My little boy made a sandcastle and ten minutes later up came this chap from the Town Hall and handed him a rates demand'.

Rivalries between boroughs are always worth exploiting – 'Of course, I always used to stay at (*wherever*), where the big knobs hang out . . .' or 'My wife first saw the light of day in Sludgeville – she was actually born two years earlier in (*wherever*) but she first saw the light of day etc., etc . . .' or 'I was wildly in love with a girl from these parts when I was a lad. I promised her I'd follow her to the ends of the earth. I would have done, too, but she moved to (*local*) . . .' or 'I used to have a cousin round here. He was a parson, doing missionary work in (*local*) . . .'

Be bold but circumspect with your ruderies – civic dignitaries may at times take their position with unwonted seriousness ('Man overboard! Man overboard!' 'Not so much of your man, my lad,' shouts the sputtering figure. 'I'm Alderman Sidebotham JP'), and citizen of a borough may not care to have their elected figurehead ridiculed too derisively. Gentle ribbing rather than apparent contempt should be the aim.

12

Coming of Age: Proposal

The proposal speech at a coming of age party usually takes
the form of a comic history of the subject's life. A magic
lantern show of pictures of the subject from the cradle to
the present day, accompanied by a humorous commentary,
takes a great deal of preparation and organization, but if
you are able to take the time and trouble to set this up it
is undoubtedly the most effective way of presenting your
speech. Alternatively, at a suitable moment you can unveil
a large blown-up photograph of the subject, taken at a
tender age and preferably in the nude.

Despite Women's Liberation, the female nature has not
changed all that much. Women are not as yet used to
having the mickey taken out of them anything like the
degree which is commonplace – and even requisite – for
boys. Readers with sons and daughters will know how
much more sensitive girls are too criticism, whether genuine
or jokey; the public, too, is not as prepared to find dero-
gation nearly as funny when directed against girls as against
boys. My experience as a Music Hall chairman has taught
me that whereas one can be as rude as one likes about male
artistes one must be very circumspect when making snide
cracks about female artistes – even when the remark may
be patently an untruth.

For instance, while it is acceptable to suggest that a girl
has lots of boy-friends, it is still definitely not acceptable –
even in fun – to suggest, in front of her parents and family,
that she sleeps around. On the other hand, if hinted at
delicately, promiscuity when linked to a male is regarded
almost as a virtue.

This attitude may be considered sexist and old-fashioned
but it is a fact of life in our society today, and a speaker
flouts convention, however hypocritical, at his peril.

*   *   *

Ladies and gentlemen, may I have your attention, please
. . . ? That's the best part of my speech so I'll say it again:
Ladies and gentlemen, may I have your attention,
please . . . ? Well, now, Brian, we are all here to congratulate you on having reached your majority and to honour the
occasion . . .[1]

I know, Brian, perhaps better than most, what a remarkable chap you are – I've heard some of the remarks . . . no,
well, Brian, you and I have known each other for many
years, we have a lot in common. Actually it's Clapham
Common we have a lot in . . . we do a lot of pulling, there[2]
The thing about you and your family, Brian, is that you
have breeding. Of course breeding isn't everything – but it's
a lot of fun, isn't it . . . ? Oh, you wouldn't know, never
mind . . . and with breeding comes good manners, and I
know you will all agree with me when I say what beautiful
manners Brian always has . . . for instance, when he dunks
his biscuits his knuckles never get wet. He is also very
generous – no, it's not true that he's suffering from an in-
growing wallet – and very kind-hearted . . . I'm not sure
what kind but it's there, anyhow. Of course it isn't surprising, because of his family background – did you know
his grandfather was a peer? Yes . . . his grandma had
kidney trouble as well, poor old duck . . .

As an infant, every morning and afternoon he'd be taken
for a walk in his pram . . . I know that wasn't much of a
walk but it kept him off the streets . . . He was remarkably
intelligent as a baby – at the age of only two and a half he
was playing on the linoleum . . . he later became an organist
but someone shot his monkey . . . He showed an early
leaning towards the bar. When his mother called upstairs
one morning, 'Brian, have you got your shoes on?' 'Yes,
Mum,' he replied, 'all except one . . .' I think that shows a
real legal brain, don't you . . . ? [3] At school his French and
Spanish were excellent, but at Algebra he was definitely
not one of the bright ones. After three years he still couldn't
say 'good evening' in it . . .

He was always a keen sportsman, of course. His favourite
sport for some time was boxing . . . do you remember that,

Brian? He was known as Kid Rembrandt, because he was always on the canvas . . . Then I well remember a cricket match in which you were batting and I was umpire. There was an appeal against you first ball – remember? – and I gave you out, 'Out?' you said, 'What for?' I said, 'For the rest of the afternoon'. Do you remember? . . . What a sportsman . . . Took it well though – didn't speak to me for three years . . .

Until he was sixteen our Brian, as many of you will know, was a boy scout. Then he became a Girl Guide . . . didn't he, Connie . . . ? [4] He went in for several scholarships and was passed by . . . a number 14 bus . . . He went to night school for a time – I met him shortly after this and said, 'What did you go in for?' He said, 'Because it was raining . . .' Always quick with the repartee, our Brian . . . then he went to medical school. I said to him, 'What are you studying there?' He said, 'I'm not – they're studying me . . .' Then for some three months he just lay around the house, singing work songs . . . (*Assuming Eamonn Andrews voice*). This was a difficult period in your young life, Brian. You decided against going into your father's business – totting [5] – but instead decided that you wanted to be a sex maniac. Again the fates were against you – you failed the medical – so you have now embarked upon a three-year City & Guilds course to become a Grade A associate member of the Combined Spot-Welders, Abattoir Operatives and Midden-Cleaners Academy.

(*Normal voice.*) But whatever you do with your life, Brian, you know that you have a loving family and a whole raft of friends to encourage and support you, just as they've always done. And when you're rich and famous . . . (*cringing and touching forelock*) you won't forget the chap who spoke up for you on your birthday will you . . . ? So I will now ask everyone to be upstanding . . . please, rise, uncle, I know it's been a long time [6] . . . and drink to Brian; congratulations, and may you live all the days of your life.

Suggested Headings

Best part of my speech.

Congratulate Brian.

Remarkable chap.

Lot in Common.

Breeding – a lot of fun.

Beautiful manners. Dunks biscuits.

Generous. Ingrowing wallet.

Grandfather was a peer.

As infant taken for walk in pram.

Intelligent. At $2\frac{1}{2}$ played on linoleum.

Organist but someone shot his monkey.

Mother:

  Got shoes on?

  All except one.

French Spanish Algebra.

Sportsman.

  Boxing: Kid Rembrandt (on canvas)

  Cricket: Out

            What for?

            Rest of the afternoon.

Boy Scout.

Scholarships. Passed by number 14 bus.

Night school. What did you go in for? Raining.

Medical school. What are you studying? Nothing. They're studying me.

Lay around house singing work songs.

Decided against family bus. Totting.

Sex maniac failed medical.

Three year course to become Grade A associate member of the Combined Spot-Welders, Abattoir Operatives & Midden-Cleaners Academy.

Whatever you do: family and friends to encourage and support.

Don't forget me when you're rich and famous.

Everyone be upstanding. I know it's been a long time.

Congratulations and may you live all the days of your life.

Notes

1. If a girl is being addressed you could add 'which used to be known as a "coming-out party" . . . and by the looks of that dress it's still not a bad name for it . . .'
2. Obviously this must be localized, and should not be used if you feel there is a chance of offence being caused.
3. This gag can be made to refer to whatever occupation the subject has decided to follow. If it is totally irrelevant, just say 'I think that showed a real shrewdness in one so young, don't you? And he'll need it in (*local firm or college*)'
4. Connie will be the acknowledged current girl friend. If any other flames are there they could all be mentioned – but be careful not to cause any tearful scenes. Remember my words on page 84 about taking the rise out of girls.
5. A friend of mine once asked me for assistance in preparing a coming-of-age speech, and I asked him, amongst many other things, what the father's occupation was. It so happened that the father was a very well-to-do furniture manufacturer. I suggested that my friend refer to this as 'totting'; he duly did so and got a positive screech of mirth. So, where appropriate, endeavour to think up an equivalently deflating description of the father's occupation or profession, i.e.: 'He decided not to join his father in the Pioneers' (where Dad is a fiercely proud Engineer or Gunner), or 'He decided not to follow in his father's footsteps and wear Her Majesty's uniform . . . he didn't think it would fit him . . .' or, 'He decided he couldn't stand the intoxicating excitement of his father's office . . .'
6. Pick on a middle-aged male relative whom you know to be a sport, otherwise don't pick on anyone in particular and just say, 'Rise, sir,' etc.

A further source of humour can be in the 'first meeting' category, e.g.: 'I first saw him some years ago when he was quite small, sitting dejectedly on the pavement on the other side of town. As I approached he started to cry, so I said, "What's the matter, sonny?" and Brian replied, "It's my birthday, and I'm having a party with jellies and cakes and ice cream and my Dad's bought me a smashing new bike with a bell on it that works!" So I said, "Well, then, why are you crying?" And he replied, "I'm bleedin' lost, ain't I?" ' . . . a characteristically direct and colourful expression.

If the father is an amiable sort of man you could also say at the beginning of your speech: 'When he was little Brian's father used to take him out in a red velveteen jacket and matching knickerbockers – he did look a scream . . .'

13

Coming of Age: Reply

Thank you, Harry [1] . . . that wasn't a speech it was an obituary . . . but it's been a marvellous eighteen years so far. It isn't true, by the way, that I was an infant prodigy. A boy genius [2] perhaps, but infant prodigy, no. I'm told that I could walk at six months – I had to, the bottom fell out of my pram . . .

But to look at me now you'd never believe that I was an ugly baby, would you? Quite incredible, isn't it . . . ? But I was so ugly Mum didn't push my pram, she used to pull it . . .

Then at school I was always very advanced, of course, very advanced. For instance when all the other kids in the class were eight I was all of fourteen . . . At school I did well in everything except lessons . . .

When I was younger we wanted for nothing in our family. All except Uncle Charlie – he was wanted for housebreaking . . . Dad always reckoned I was going to be a waiter when I grew up – he said I never came when he called . . . Then I started going out with girls. I started doing that as soon as I found out they weren't boys . . . then I went for my first job – at (local).[3] The manager offered me £20 a week now and another £10 in six months. So I told him I'd be back in six months . . .

By the way, for those of you still wondering what to get an eighteen-year-old boy – how about a seventeen-year-old girl . . . ? [4]

I'd like to thank Sis for baking the cake – it's what I call her Enthusiasm Cake. She puts everything she's got into it . . .

Being eighteen I can now vote, of course. Dad asked me whether I would vote for the Tories or the Socialists. I said I'd have to wait and see because I didn't know much about either – well, I mean, they haven't had anything in the charts lately, have they? . . . Being now an adult means I can do a lot of other marvellous things I couldn't do as a child, like going bankrupt, joining the Army, getting hanged for treason, and so on . . . yes, it sure is fun being grown-up.

I'd like to thank you all most sincerely for honouring the occasion with your presence, and special thanks to those who bought me presents . . . and to those who didn't – GET OUT! No, just my little joke [5] . . . And of course, lastly and most importantly, I must thank my parents – for having me. Thank you.

Suggested Headings

Not a speech, an obituary.
Not true that I was an infant prodigy – boy genius.
Could walk at six months. Bottom out of pram.
Used to be ugly – Mum used not to push but to pull.
At school always very advanced. Kids 8 when I was 14.
Did well in everything except lessons.
Wanted for nothing in family.
Except Uncle Charlie – wanted for housebreaking.
Dad reckoned I would be a waiter – I never came when he called.
Started going out with girls when I found out they weren't boys.
First job : at (local) £20 p.w. and another £10 in six months.
What to get for 18 year old boy.
Sis made Enthusiasm Cake.
Being 18 can now vote. Tories or Socialists. Also can go bankrupt, join Army, be hanged, etc.
Thanks for coming, especially for presents.
Thank parents for having me.

Notes

1. Harry is of course the name of the previous speaker. Check this speech beforehand, because if it is not comic you must not use this first gag. If it is very sincere and

sentimental, say instead, 'Thanks, Harry – I thought you were talking about someone else' which will break the mood without making Harry look foolish.

2. For boy read girl if applicable, although frankly I don't think an eighteen-year-old girl should attempt a comic speech on such an occasion. I am no male chauvinist, but it should be remembered that such a speech will inevitably be accompanied by a good deal of barracking and chi-iking and it seems to me quite unfitting for a young girl to be the target for such raillery, however affectionate and good-natured it might be. Boys and men are accustomed to taking the micky out of each other – this is very much a male characteristic – but the opposite sex, being naturally more gentle, is not. And so, while I am by no means against the idea of ladies being comical, I consider that a comic speech by a girl at her coming-of-age party would be inappropriate.

3. This could be a local firm notorious for its rough working conditions of ill-useage of its work-force, or a firm specializing in work which violently contrasts with the speaker's actual work or study course.

4. Obviously if there is a girl-friend in evidence this gag will be cut.

5. 'No, just my little joke' to be said bitterly between clenched teeth à la John Cleese.

Your choice of occupation should be mentioned in your speech, especially if the proposer of your health has dwelt on the subject. You can introduce it by saying, 'Actually I wanted to emigrate as soon as I found out I couldn't be King . . . but now etc.' A jokey reference to your reaching the top of the tree always goes down well – i.e. if you are studying law you might say 'Thank you for saying what a fine lawyer I'll make, but I'm not the President of the Law Society . . . yet!' One instance of this approach was given by a friend of mine who was about to take his final orders as a Roman Catholic priest. 'I'm not infallible,' he said, '. . . yet!'

References to siblings, if any, or close cousins, should be

made, i.e., 'I used to pray to God every night to make Sis a good girl, but after ten years I gave it up as a lost cause.' This can also be inverted as though Sis had said it about you. Similarly:

'I asked Sis if she could help me with my maths homework. She said no because it wouldn't be right. I said I knew that but she could at least try . . .'

'Shortly after I was born, I'm told my brother asked Mum if I had come from heaven. Mum told him that I had, whereupon my affectionate brother said, "Well, I don't blame the angels for chucking him out!" '

'I remember one day after tea when we had been fighting like cat and dog we were both sent to bed in disgrace. We were lying on our beds in the back bedroom upstairs and I thought I'd try to make up, so I whispered "are you awake?" And a small sulky voice said," Not telling you!" '

'I well remember how upset Sis was when she made a steak and kidney pie and the cat ate it. But I comforted her, as a brother should. I said, "Don't worry, Sis. Dad will buy us another cat . . . !" '

'I once asked Grandad if he had been in Noah's Ark. "No," he said, so then I asked him why he hadn't been drowned . . .'

'I once saw Mum at the mirror pulling out some grey hairs. "Look at that!" she said, "I'm going grey. That's because you're such a bad boy to me." I said. "Gosh, Mum, you must have been awful to Grandma!" '

'I once asked Mum whether God used our bathroom. "No," she said, "why do you ask?' I said, 'Because this morning I heard Dad knock on the bathroom door and say, "Oh, God, are you still in there?" '

Be careful about mentioning friends in your speech – anyone left out with any kind of claim to recognition may be offended. Be tactful in your family references, also, it is probably safest to restrict names to those in your immediate household.

Where appropriate thank your parents or whoever is paying for the food and drink. Thanks are also due for 'the use of the hall' if the party is not being held in your own family home.

14

Engagement: Proposal

Your attention, ladies and gentlemen, please – your attention . . . What are you all staring at? . . . Now, you know
the purpose of this meeting so I'll not keep you long. It is,
of course, formally to announce the engagement of my
daughter, Deirdre, to er . . . er . . . what was your name
again? . . . Bruce, of course! So sorry . . . the engagement
of my daughter Deirdre to Bruce.

He's a nice lad and my wife and I are delighted with
Deirdre's choice. He's a bit old-fashioned, but none the
worse for that. No, I respect the old ways – after all he
came to me very properly and said, 'Sir . . .' I thought
'Who's he talking to? He usually says "Oi, you!"' Anyway, he said, 'Sir, I have the honour to ask for your daughter's hand.' You did, didn't you, Bruce? So I said, 'Sorry,
son – it goes with the set . . .' So that's why they're getting
married . . . personally I wouldn't trust him with a double-
breasted jacket, but then that's not my problem . . . Anyway I then said to him, 'So you want to be my son-in-law,
do you?' He said, 'Not really, but if I want to marry
Deirdre I haven't got much choice, have I?' Which I
thought was a very fair answer, very fair . . . Your face has
all healed up now, Bruce, has it? . . . Good.

Of course this event has not been entirely unexpected in
certain quarters – for some time now Jack [1] has been referring to Bruce as 'Yoyo', because he's been kept dangling
on a string . . . I'm really going to embarrass Deirdre now
and tell you, Bruce, about her first kiss. She was eleven
and a half and her teeth were in braces; the boy concerned
also had his teeth in braces – we had to call in the fire
brigade to get 'em apart . . . I thought that might have
cured you, Deirdre, but I suppose it hasn't . . .

Naturally like any father I am concerned with my future
son-in-law's prospects so one day I asked Deirdre what

Bruce earned. Do you know what she replied? She said, 'That's funny, Dad, he's asked me the same question about you . . .' But I know, Bruce, you were very worried about my attitude to this proposed union – after all, it isn't every father who would welcome a Yorkshireman into the family [2] – although you needn't have concerned yourself. When Deirdre told me she wanted to get engaged I was delighted . . . mind you, I always am delighted . . . I won't say she dropped any hints to him but all last summer she was fanning him with a marriage licence . . .

But it brings it all back to me – many years ago, Deirdre, before I met your mother I thought I was madly in love with this girl but I couldn't pluck up the courage to propose. Finally I got so desperate – I telephoned her! 'Darling!' I said, 'will you marry me?' And she said, 'Of course I will, you mad, headstrong fool you – who is it speaking?'

I must admit, with the best will in the world, I can't quite see what it is that Deirdre is so starry-eyed about. I asked her the other day and she said, 'Oh, he sends me.' I said. 'But I thought Rod McKuen sent you?' [3] She said, 'Oh, he does, but not so far . . .' Well, whatever it is, he's got it . . . now young man, we don't want a long engagement – I want to give you a daughter, not a pension . . .

I realize finding somewhere to live is the biggest headache. One young chap I know wanted to get married and had this problem, so I said to him, 'What about living with your parents for a year or two?' He said, 'That's no good – they're still living with *their* parents . . .'

Of course, the advantage to staying single is that you can get out of bed either side but apart from that I firmly believe that the married state is the best way for people to live and . . . (*looking at notes*) . . . it says here . . . no, I mean it – I'm all for the institution of marriage and I know we all are looking forward to the calling of the banns. Oh no, in fact there won't be any banns, just a concertina after tea . . . so until the happy day let us drink to Deirdre and Bruce and thank Providence, as I am sure they do, for having brought them together. To Deirdre and Bruce!

Suggested Headings

Attention – staring at?
Purpose of meeting.
What was your name again?
Wife and I delighted – old fashioned.
Sir . . . daughter's hand . . . goes with the set.
Doublebreasted jacket.
Want to be my son-in-law . . . not much choice.
Face all healed up?
Yoyo.
First kiss – braces – fire brigade.
I asked D how much B earned.
Not every father would welcome a Yorkshireman.
When D told me I was delighted . . . always am.
Fanning him with a marriage licence.
Telephoned proposal . . . who is speaking, please?
D: he sends me. Rod McKuen? Yes, but not so far.
Not long engagement – give you daughter not pension.
Somewhere to live – with parents.
Advantage to staying single.
Calling of the banns . . . concertina after tea . . .
Thank Providence.

Notes

1. Jack will be a sibling of the bride-to-be – preferably a younger one.
2. This can be varied at will – obviously 'Yorkshireman' is only a jokey insult in Lancashire; City versus United football clubs are alternatives, 'North Road Comprehensive boy' is another, this being the school with a bad local reputation. But don't try to be Alf Garnett by using such descriptives as 'wog' or 'dago', which will simply freeze everyone with horror.

The prospective son-in-law's occupation is another source of gentle ribbing – if he does something rather obscure in the Civil Service you can say, 'I don't really know what he does but I believe it's so hush-hush he isn't at all sure what he's doing himself . . .' If he's in the

Army call him a Pongo and say 'thank God for the Navy . . .' If he's in the Navy say, 'It must be very exciting to be in the Navy – all those rowlocks and bollards and things . . .'

Habits may be mentioned – if you are known for your beer consumption you might say, 'It isn't every father who would welcome a gin-drinker into the family . . .' Pipe-smoking versus roll-ups, television programmes, preferred newspapers – all these are possible sources of hilarity.

3. Rod McKuen will of course be replaced by the latest rave, who should be someone your daughter most definitely does *not* like, thus provoking a shriek of protest from her and an extra laugh from the company.

Keep this speech brief and very light-hearted; don't dwell on anecdotes of Deirdre's childhood or how long you've known Bruce's parents etc., etc., since this approach belongs to your speech on the wedding day itself, which is a far more solemn occasion.

15

Engagement: Reply

Thank you, everyone, and thank you, Mr. Splurge, for
those very . . . er . . . for those er . . . for speaking. I must
apologize for the absence of my old friend, Jim Crint, who
unfortunately can't be with us tonight [1] – I believe he's
helping the police with their enquiries . . . wonderful to
see you all here . . . or most of you . . . it's a funny coincidence but when I told Ralph over there that I was getting
engaged [2] he said, 'Really? Yesterday I got *my* girl to say
yes.' I said, 'Marvellous – when's the wedding?' He said,
'What wedding . . . ?'

It's all very well for you to laugh, Dave – I've heard all
about you. Do you know, last year Dave sent his picture
off to a Lonely Hearts Club and they sent it back [3] . . . said
they weren't that lonely.

Anyway, ladies and gentlemen, I'm sure you would all
agree that I'm a good judge of women. I can tell a woman
from a man every time . . . or nearly every time . . . There
have been some interesting errors now and again . . .

But Deirdre's such a great girl – I think I'm so lucky.
She's kind, warm-hearted, generous – just like her father
. . . Naturally I did the right thing and asked his permis-
sion. I said to him, 'May I have your daughter for my wife?'
He said, 'No – tell her to get one of her own . . .' I said,
'But I want to marry her.' He said, 'Oh, I get you now.
Have you seen my wife?' I said, 'Yes, but she's already
married . . .'

So when we got all that sorted out he said we must celebrate, so he got out a bottle of his home-made wine [4] . . .
(*roll eyes to heaven and give the slightest suggestion of
nausea*) . . . but I'm all right now . . . anyway, I took a swig
and – well, it really was awful! Ghastly taste! He said,
'Well, what do you think of that?' Well, I thought, I must
be honest – you know, start as you mean to go on, so I said,

'Well, I'm sorry, Pop . . . but frankly, it's very bitter, isn't it?' So he took a swig and spat it out and said, 'You're right, it is . . . I'll kill that cat . . . !' Actually, that's a joke I usually only tell at funerals, because you have to be a little stiff to appreciate it . . .

But I know I'm going to get along fine with my in-laws – not like a pal of mine. One day his wife said to him, 'Now look here, your mother has been living with us for six years now and she's driving me up the wall. I'm sorry but she's got to go!' And my pal said, '*My* mother? But I thought she was *your* mother . . . !'

Do you know where Deirdre and I met? It was at the fair on (*local*) common – in the Tunnel of Love . . . she was digging. I didn't waste any time, mind you – by the time we came out I'd developed four rolls of film . . . When we'd been going out for about a year I knew something was up because when I picked Deirdre up one evening she suddenly burst into tears, – didn't you, love? – and she said, 'I'm going to wind up an old maid!' I thought, 'That's a funny way to spend an evening, but still . . .' So I thought I'd save her from a fate worse than a fate worse than death, and here we are.

Needless to say my parents are thrilled that I'm marrying into such a weal – such a nice family. My Mum's been giving Dierdre a crash course on how to tie my shoe-laces . . . and my Dad's gone into training for all the supping that's to be done at the wedding – how are you doing, Dad? . . . strewth – half past nine and he's still upright [5] . . .

I hope everyone's admired the ring . . . contrary to popular belief it hasn't been used before. Nice, isn't it? . . . marvellous what you can get on Green Shield stamps. Mind you, I've been saving for that ring for fifteen years ever since I saw Raquel Welch in 'Planet of the Apes' . . . and it broke my heart when I found out she was married to a gorilla [6] . . . Still, Deirdre's had her moments, too, you know. Robert Redford's given her a few sleepless nights, I can tell you [7] . . .

But anyway, I know you want to get on with some dancing and prancing, and we've got a new single poised on the turn-table; it's the pawnbroker's song – 'For You Alone' – so I'll just finish up by saying I've got the girl, she's got the ring, and we know that we both have your good wishes and your love – and without that we can't go far wrong. Thank you.

Suggested Headings

Thank you for those few . . . words.

Apologize for Jim Crint – helping police.

Coincidence. Ralph. Got my girl to say yes.

Dave. Lonely Hearts Club.

I'm a good judge of women.

Deirdre's kind, warm-hearted, generous.

Asked her father's permission.

May I have your daughter for my wife? No, tell her to get one of her own.

Have you seen my wife? Already married.

Home-made wine. Ghastly taste. Bitter. Kill that cat.

Pal of mine's wife: your mother with us for six years.

Deirdre and I met in Tunnel of Love. Digging. Developed four rolls of film.

I'll wind up an old maid.

My parents thrilled. Mum giving Deirdre crash course.

Dad's gone into training for all the supping. 9.30 and he's still upright.

Everyone admired the ring? Hasn't been used . . . Green Shield stamps.

Saving for 15 years since seeing Raquel Welch in 'Planet of the Apes'.

Broke my heart. Married to gorilla.

Deirdre's had her moments too. Robert Redford.

Dancing and prancing. New single. Pawnbroker's song 'For You Alone'.

I've got the girl. She's got the ring.

We've both got your good wishes and love can't go far wrong.

Notes

It would be absurd for me to pretend that the above represents anything other than the vaguest outline or blue-print for a speech in reply to the toast of 'The Engaged Couple'. Obviously every family condition and circumstance varies – for instance I have not mentioned any siblings on either side ('Her younger brother's been very friendly to me since I gave him a Spurs scarf for his birthday' – this sort of thing is always good for a laugh when everyone present knows that the boy is a fanatical Chelsea fan). In fact the engagement party could very well be held miles away from the families of either affianced, in which case the speech suggested here won't be a lot of use to you.

1. There is always someone who can't get to any party whose name will be well known to the majority of those present.
2. 'Ralph' will be the local Don Juan.
3. 'Dave' will be an aspiring Don Juan. Don't pick on any boy who is actually poorly regarded by the girls – that would be too cruel.
4. Home-made wine can be altered to whatever your future father-in-law's pet hobby happens to be, with the rest of the story altered to suit. ('He invited me to play a couple of rounds of golf, so I said to him, 'Tell me, Pop, if I were to marry your daughter, what would you give me?' He thought a bit and then said, 'I'll give you the next two holes ... !')
5. You will know your own father better than me, so you will know whether this crack will be appropriate. A word of warning: if you wish to be rude about your own father in public, the most likely person to be offended will be your mother ...
6. This reference must neccessarily be a very personalized one; the star or starlet to be remembered should be some slightly passée sex symbol in her most famous role.
7. Robert Redford would be the male equivalent ... Paul Newman might be another.

Notice that this speech is as clean as a whistle. I have written for a family gathering; references to sex will only embarrass the aunts and grannies – not to mention the Mums and Dads – since engaged couples are still conventionally not supposed to indulge in the Great Pastime. Keep the blue material for the Stag Party.

16

Farewell Party: Proposal

Ladies and gentlemen . . . (*louder*) Ladies and gentlemen!
. . . have I missed anyone out . . . ? No? . . . some of you
not so sure? Oh well . . . as you know, this wake has been
convened so that we might bid a fond farewell to our
greatly esteemed colleague and friend, so well-known and
much loved by us all . . . (*sotto*) . . . what was the name
again? Oh yes . . . So Stephen [1] . . . we don't want to lose
you but we think . . . (*pause to allow the company to finish
off with 'you ought to go'*)

So as you tread life's path – or in your case I should
say 'shamble' along life's path in the great world outside the
Processing Department [2] . . . let your thoughts turn back to
us from time to time. Think of George still trying to get last
Wednesday's balance right [3] . . . think of Maria still trying
to get the office mugs clean [4] . . . think of Arthur – no, better
not to think of Arthur, ever. Think of Rosie instead, that's
much more fun [5] . . .

Well, Stuart, we shall miss your merry quips and witty
puns [6] . . . your gay carolling about the corridors and in the
office . . . your ever smiling, sunny nature which never
deserted you . . . not even when Sadie dropped the telephone on your foot [7] . . .

Who can forget the day you and Jack discovered an error
in the estimates and you both had to work over an entire
and very hot week-end? But did you complain, Simon . . . ?
(*turning to the company*) Did he complain? He – cried like
a baby [8]. . .

As a going away present, Sandy, Joyce thought she'd do
your picture in oils [9] . . . But after she'd dropped your
photograph in the chip pan it seemed to go all soggy, so
we abandoned that idea; then we thought you might like a
life-size statue of the managing director done in raspberry
jelly, but then we remembered how much you dislike rasp-

berries so we had to think again, and we asked your family.[10]

Your family will miss you even more than we will, of course. I understand your Mum is having your room fumi – decorated, and (*turning to the company*) if anyone would like four hundred copies of the Spanking and Bondage Gazette they can call round any time ...

But it's wonderful to travel, isn't it? You're so lucky, Sean ... I love being abroad ... mind you, tonight I'm a chap ... But I really do enjoy being in foreign parts ... it reminds me of my youth, I suppose – he joined the Navy[11] ... It really is a most exciting place you're going to. I've been there myself, as it happens, and I like it ... as a whole ... I spent a year there – one Wednesday afternoon ... but things really are looking up in that part of the world. I'm told they're sending missionaries there now from Neasden [12] ... it's said that travel broadens the mind – but if his broadens any more it'll be flat as a pan-cake ...

And watch the women in that part of the world, Solly ... be a good boy, now, won't you? (*To the company*) I said to him earlier, 'Now, Sylvester, would you endanger your immortal soul for an hour of animal passion?' To which he replied, 'How do you make it last an hour ... ?' But I know he's a careful lad. He's so cautious he even looks both ways before crossing his legs. I'm not sure what that means, either ... But anyway, Sebastian, you've certainly made your mark in your time with us ... Doris has tried everything to get it out [13] ... and your departure will leave a big gap in our lives. Harry will now be able to throw his gas mask away – not that he minded you smoking a pipe or cigarettes or cigars ... it was when you started smoking bacon that he thought things had got a little out of hand. With your going the days will seem a little longer and darker for all of us ... I think without you, a little something will die in this office ... well, no-one else is going to feed that snake ... '

So to the presentation. First of all, Sam, here is a card with all our signatures on it – even Johnny's. He had special coaching from Daphne [14] ... Having consulted your family, and having discussed it at great length between ourselves, and knowing your passion for asphalt-laying [15] . . . we thought you'd like a 5lb tin of rat poison . . . and a year's supply of rats . . . but then we decided instead to get you something rather more decorative (*or practical or whatever is appropriate*). Use it in good health – and think of us. (*Hand over the gift and shake hands*) From all of us, the very best of good fortune, every success and happiness, and – it's been nice knowing you.[16]

Suggested Headings

L & G – missed anyone out?

Stephen – we don't want to lose you, but . . .

Shamble along life's path. Think of us.

George. Last Wednesday's balance.

Maria – office mugs.

Arthur. Rosie.

Stuart. We shall miss your quips and puns and gay carolling.

Ever smiling sunny nature. Sadie. Dropped telephone.

You and Jack discovered error in the estimates.

Did Simon complain?

Joyce. Picture in oils.

Life-size statue of MD in raspberry jelly.

Mum having your room fumi – decorated.

400 back copies of Spanking & Bondage Gazette.

Wonderful to travel. So lucky Sean.

I love being abroad.

Foreign parts.

Reminds me of my youth.

Exciting place you are going to – I spent a year there.

Things are looking up. Missionaries from (*local*).

Travel broadens the mind.

Watch women there. Would you endanger your immortal soul for an hour of animal passion? How do you make it last an hour?

So cautious he looks both ways before crossing his legs.

Sebastian you've made your mark. Doris has tried everything.

Your departure a big gap.

Harry throw away gas mask. Smoking (bacon).

Without you a little something will die.

Presentation. Card with sigs – even Johnny's. Coaching from Daphne.

Knowing your passion for asphalt-laying.

5lb tin of rat poison and year's supply of rats.

Something more decorative.

Use it in good health and think of us.

From all of us, the very best of good fortune, every success and happiness, and it's been nice knowing you.

Notes

As is apparent, this speech is primarily designed as the blueprint for an office farewell gathering. It can, however, be adapted for other venues, and shows the general lines to be followed.

1. This is a running joke through the speech: the subject's name is in fact, shall we say, Silas, and you get it wrong every time you have to say it.
2. Obviously, the 'Processing Department' stands for whatever situation or location the subject is in.
3. George trying to get last Wednesday's balance right – this can be adapted to incorporate any debacle still fresh in people's minds.
4. Maria will be the junior, responsible for the tea and coffee delivery round the office. She has perhaps been chided for not washing up properly.
5. Arthur will be the office goon or clown, and Rosie will be the office glamour-queen.
6. Quips and puns – the subject is perhaps notorious for making awful jokes. His gay carolling might refer to an extremely loud and tuneless voice.
7. Sadie dropping the telephone: this bizzare incident you will possibly be able to adapt to any untoward incident in which your subject was involved.

8. This could be another well-known anecdote in your subject's checkered career. If you can't think of anything suitable, just invent some outrageous exploit, i.e. 'Who can ever forget the time he came in wearing a kilt upside down and said he was going to a fancy-dress party as a shuttlecock? Incidentally, I heard that Rosie was also at that party – all she wore was a pair of black boots and a pair of black gloves. Nothing else . . . she went as the five of spades . . .'

9. Joyce could be the artistic one in the office, or the one who always does caricatures of office personnel.

10. All the references to family will need to be revised if the family is not readily consultable, i.e. if the subject is from distant parts.

11. All these jokes will need to be varied or even omitted if the subject is not in fact leaving for abroad, but most of the material is quite easily adjusted. The mode of travel to be used by the subject can be a source of comedy, i.e. if by air: 'The last time I travelled in one of their aircraft it had an outside loo . . .' If by sea: 'That's a marvellous line – the toilet rolls on board are two inches wider than usual to allow for the roll of the ship . . .'

12. Neasden: this is only effective if the towns or districts referred to are well known to all present. If the subject is leaving for, say, the Dispatch Department within the same firm, missionaries can be sent from Accounts.

13. Doris will be the cleaner.

14. Daphne can be either one of the girls known to have a soft spot for your subject, or she can be a motherly earthy soul who is always good for a shriek; alternatively she can be someone extremely august and senior – one of the directors or an extremely tough and unpopular departmental head ('Daphne' does not have to be female).

15. Asphalt-laying: or anything as wildly ludicrous or incongruous. If your subject is a noted beer drinker you can refer to a passion for barley water.

16. If there is alcohol available, you will finish with a toast finally getting the name right!

Laughter is not at all a bad beginning for a friendship, and it is far the best ending for one. *Oscar Wilde.*

17

Farewell Party: Reply

It is vital for you to check the proposer's speech before-hand. If you want to be funny you *must* know what he is going to say; he may well be using similar if not identical gags, and as he is to speak first you could very well find the ground cut out from under your feet with about four minutes flat to think up alternative hilarities. Don't be coy about it – ring him up a couple of days before the party and ask him outright.

*　　　　*　　　　*

Thank you. The first thing I was to say is that this is National Sex week, so if you give here at the office you don't have to give at home ...

I'd like to say how great it's been working with you all ... I'd like to but I can't – no! ... you've really been a grand bunch. A grand bunch ... like half a ton of Fyffe's ... and I'm really going to miss you all. I understand that if I'd stayed on I might have been in the running for the Euphemia Caldigate Trophy for Keeping Cheerful Under Adversity [1] ... but the call of the great outdoors cannot be denied. So when you are beavering away in this nice, modern, warm, clean, air-conditioned, well-appointed, comfortable, superbly-designed office [2] ... think of me lying under a palm tree in Fiji and – eat your hearts out ..

I must thank all those who have been so kind and con-siderate to me – my immediate colleagues Bill and Ben the Chamberpot Men [3] ... two lads who made allowances for my rough, ignorant, uncouth ways when I first arrived here and helped to instil a little polish, grace and courtliness into my demeanour. I appreciated their attention because before coming here I was a garlic salesman and I'd been extremely lonely, so it was wonderful to find everyone so friendly ... weren't you, Rita? [4] Bill showed me where everything was, Ben showed me the Club Bar, Bill showed me the canteen, Ben showed me the Greyhound, Bill showed me the wash-room, Ben showed me the Hare and Hounds . . . It was those two boys who showed me the correct angle of declination required when bowing to Ming the Merciless [5] . . .

Mr Tuglock,[6] I must also thank you for being so patient with all my shortcomings. It never seemed to worry you, no matter how late I arrived in the mornings – perhaps because you never noticed; after all you carry a big responsibility keeping the rubber plants washed [7] . . . Even when I put a joke mouse on the conveyor belt in Packaging and the entire shop-floor went on strike for three hours you did not upbraid me. You just stood there, and – cried . . .

I'd like to take this opportunity of thanking Sir Filthy Lucre [8] who unfortunately can't be with us – he's on late turn – without whose help, advice and persuasive charm I might still be – staying on . . .

Finally I'd like most especially to thank Rita for furthering my education in the liberal arts. If I'd stayed another week I think I might have finished the course . . . another of life's 'might-have-beens' . . .

I did go for a job at a strip club, applying the girls' body makeup, £30 a week – I know it wasn't much but I still couldn't afford it. Then I thought about becoming a dustman – £40 a week and as much as you could eat. I nearly joined a circus – mucking out fifteen elephants . . . too heavy for me . . . so I've decided to take a job which will give me some opportunities to travel. I'll be looking for gas leaks with lighted matches . . .

Finally, folks, thank you very much indeed for the card and the present. When I left my last job they gave me a jumbo-sized tin of beans – I was deeply moved . . . but I'm sure you've got more imagination. (*Open present and make suitable remark.*) Wonderful, that's really great of you. Boys and girls, it's been great knowing and working with you all, and as the poet says:

Some weep because they part,
And languish broken-hearted.
And others – Oh, my heart! –
Because they never parted! [9]

Suggested Headings

National Sex Week.

Grand bunch.

Euphemia Caldigate Trophy for Keeping Cheerful Under Adversity.

Call of great outdoors cannot be denied when you are beavering.

Bill and Ben the Chamberpot Men.

Used to be a garlic salesman.

Everyone so friendly – weren't you, Rita?

Bill and Ben showed me around. And how to bow to Ming the Merciless.

Mr. Tuglock never worried when I was late. Washing rubber plants. Even when I put joke mouse on belt.

Sir Filthy Lucre on late turn. Might still be staying on.

Thank Rita for furthering my ed in liberal arts.

Strip club applying make-up. £30 a week but too much.

Dustman – £40 a week and as much as you could eat.

Circus mucking out elephants. Too heavy.

Job with travel opportunities looking for gas leaks with lighted match.

Finally thanks for card and present. Last job they gave me jumbo tin of beans.

Some weep because they part.
And languish broken-hearted.
And others – Oh, my heart –
Because they never parted,

Notes

1. 'Euphemia Caldigate' will be someone in authority and the trophy for 'Keeping Cheerful Under Adversity' will refer to some pet phrase or saying for which this person

112

is well-known. Or it could refer to someone's known prejudices or predilections, i.e. 'The Chloroform Wiggins Challenge Bowl for Positive Thinking'.

2. Each adjective should be interspersed with a long pause to enable your audience to jeer and make suitable comments thereon.

3. Bill and Ben will be two young men who are known to be close friends. If it is clear to whom you are referring you could actually call them Bill and Ben the Chamber-pot Men rather than their real names.

4. Rita is of course the girl strongly rumoured to have a crush on you. If you are female change to an appropriate male name; don't use the name of the office groper since it will only encourage him to pester the unfortunate female who will be taking your job.

5. Ming the Merciless will be any unpopular authoritarian superior.

6. Mr. Tuglock will be a popular easy-going supervisor or manager.

7. The reference to rubber plants you will replace with mention of well-known foible or mild eccentricity – *cf* Captain Queeg and the missing strawberries.

8. Sir Filthy Lucre will be the chairman of the board or the managing director or the boss man of the whole shebang. I once used this quip ('he's on late turn') at a gathering of BBC employees – I was on the staff myself at the time – and referred to the then Director-General. It got a scream.

9. Write out the poem in full on your headings cards. Under the stress of the moment you might forget it, which would be a dreadful anti-climax. Alternatively, omit the poem altogether, especially if the present has over-whelmed you. These occasions can be very emotional for the recipient, which makes everyone else a touch weepy as well, so don't feel you have to finish on a boffo laugh.

I haven't really funked it by writing 'open present and make suitable remark', since I cannot know what present you will be given. But you can perhaps find out beforehand and devise a suitable comment – it doesn't have to be a funny one – to be delivered quietly and sincerely to show your appreciation of the thought, time and effort which has gone into the presentation.

18

Guest of Honour: Proposal

Ladies and gentlemen – what do you think of the evening so far [1] ... ? Isn't it warm, though? Do you know, on my way here I distinctly saw a tree chasing a dog [2] ... As you know, we have only one speaker: the remainder of the evening will be given over to pure enjoyment.

Well, now, we are met to do honour to and to welcome into our midst a man who, despite his singular accomplishments and attainments, has remained remarkably modest. But then if we examine his life in detail, we can see that he has a lot to be modest about. He came from Scunthorpe – a move which shows an acute perception for a start [3] ... He was educated at Harrow ... Secondary Modern ... where he did extremely well, getting a very near miss in both his O levels [4] and also getting an even closer Miss on the level behind the gasworks ...

On leaving school he endeavoured to join the Royal Air Force, until the medics discovered his unfortunate propensity to haemorrhage at altitude. He even got a nose-bleed wearing platforms ... In the Army however he did very well; after three years' service he reached the rank of private, third class, smoking. But it was in the Navy that his career was really spectacular – within one year of signing on he was Chief Petting Officer for the Home Fleet.

He then knocked about the world a bit, sowing his wild oats ... and every Sunday praying for a crop failure. In Canada he became the only man ever to go up Niagara Falls in a barrel; in America he became a telegraph linesman – but it drove him up the pole. In Australia he teamed up with a stripper ... she'd strip the lead off the roofs and he'd sell it. In South Africa he became a lighthouse-keeper – but after a time it got on his wick. So, back in Britain, he became an actor. You've heard of King Lear? Our guest played his brother – Chandelier. But he soon left that – too much hanging about. Mind you, in Shakespeare he was

115

well known for his portrayal in 'A Midsummer Night's Dream'. His Bottom is still well remembered . . . definitely his finest part. Then he decided to become a salesman, but being a very independent sort of person he couldn't take orders from anyone. He then served for some time as a missionary to (*local*), before seeing the light and returning to civilization to join the firm of Lock, Stock and Barrel.[5] Since when, in a remarkably brief space of time he has risen mightily in our regard and respect.

Last year, as you all know, he was awarded – by unanimous consent of the panel – the Mary Whitehouse Plaque for the Man Most Likely To Keep A Firm Grip On Himself. He also won a coveted seat on the – 8.45 from Euston [6] . . . he just pipped an old lady on crutches . . . and this year he has won £25 on his premium bonds.

So now we see him, a self-made man – and *that's* a good trick if you can do it . . . you'd need to be a contortionist, I should think. So now we see him loaded with honours, with fame, with wealth . . . and from the look of him tonight, just plain loaded.

While I think of it, we want to make him feel well and truly at home, so I'd like to introduce a custom here tonight which is practised as a matter of course in his own home town. When I introduce him, as well as applauding or cheering or whistling or throwing up – no! – I want you to stamp your feet. This is apparently the custom in Scunthorpe (*or wherever*), so shall we have a little rehearsal? (*start everyone stamping*) . . . thank you – we're having a lot of trouble with cockroaches at the moment . . .

It therefore gives me great pleasure – not that my private life is any concern of yours – to ask you all to rise . . . well, do your best, Charlie, I know it's been a long time [7] . . . and drink the health of our esteemed and thrice-welcome guest: the man who has been described as one of this country's leading (*whatever*), and here is the man who said it: Roger Fudgeknuckle!

Suggested Headings

What do you think of the evening so far?
Warm. Tree chasing a dog.
One speaker only.
We are all met to honour (*name*). Modest.
Came from Scunthorpe.
Educated at Harrow.
Very near miss in both his O levels and an even closer miss on the level behind the gasworks.
RAF. Haemorrhage/platforms.
Army. Private 3rd class smoking.
Navy Chief Petting Officer for the Home Fleet.
Then he knocked about sowing wild oats/crop failure.
Canada. Up Niagara Falls.
USA. Telegraph linesman/up the pole.
Australia. Joined up with stripper.
S. Africa. Lighthouse keeper/got on his wick.
Britain. Actor – King Lear/Chandelier/hanging about/Dream/Bottom.
Salesman but too independent. Couldn't take orders.
Missionary to (*local*).
Mary Whitehouse Plaque for the Man Most Likely To Keep A Firm Grip On Himself.
Seat on the 8.45 from Euston/pipped old lady.
£25 premium bonds.
Self-made man – good trick.
Loaded.
Stamping routine.
All rise – do your best Charlie.
One of this country's rising young (*whatever*).

Notes

If your guest of honour is genuinely distinguished, it is not advisable to deliver a speech which is unreservedly joke-denigratory. The Eminent tend to have even larger and more sensitive egos than we ordinary mortals – that is precisely one of the things which helps towards making them eminent in the first place. In such an instance, keep

117

the jokes minimal and expand the 'but seriously' closing section. Another thing to remember about introducing the great and famous: their very presence casts lustre upon everyone there, and the more you point up the guest's qualifications for immortality and eventual interment in Westminster Abbey the more you will be underlining your auditors' own importance and distinction which is always a very agreeable experience. It is a subtle form of flattery, and a very effective one, for reflected glory can be almost as bright as the real thing.

1. 'The evening' will of course be altered to suit – 'the party' or 'the dinner', etc. This question will be immediately followed by a general shout of 'Rubbish!' which gives everyone a good laugh and gets you off to an excellent start, so make sure you are heard from the very beginning by repeating 'Ladies and gentlemen' a couple of times.
2. The 'tree chasing a dog' may seem contrived but in my experience this elicits a far bigger laugh than the joke would appear to warrant. If on the other hand it is cold you might say, 'I passed a brass monkey looking distinctly worried'.
3. 'Scunthorpe' should either be the actual birthplace of the guest if it suits or an area known for its unlovableness.
4. It is best to refer to O levels for the sake of the second reference to 'level' although if required this gag can be adapted to other examination boards.
5. 'Lock Stock & Barrel' should obviously be the name of the guest's firm, if appropriate, or alternatively his profession or calling.
6. This train should be altered to suit local conditions.
7. This scornful and extremely derisory reference should be made only if you are quite sure that 'Charlie' will take it in what is generally referred to as 'the right spirit'!

19

Guest of Honour: Reply

Thank you. May you live as long as those jokes. It is really very sweet and groovy of you [1] to say all that about me, but I think you ought to know that no pro would ever turn down the chance of a free meal.[2] As it happens I was nearly late arriving – my car had a flat tyre. I was changing the wheel by the roadside just out of town at . . . er, what's it called?, that pretty little spot – Slagview, that's it . . . anyway, I was just lifting the wheel off when up came this chap, a total stranger, and he opened up the bonnet and started fiddling about inside. I said, 'Hey – what are you doing?' And he said, 'Well, if you're having the wheels I'm having the battery . . .' Enterprising round here, aren't they . . . ?

But it's really splendid to be here. The dinner was marvellous – did you all enjoy the dinner . . . ? It's such a pity I have to spoil it for you now . . . have you ever thought what a strange custom this business of after-dinner speaking is? After all, we are unique in the animal kingdom in this respect – all other animals, after a good feed, have the sense to lie down and have a kip . . . (*yawn*) ah, well . . .

I must thank your committee for having invited me. In most clubs like this half the committee do all the work and the other half do nothing at all. I'm happy to tell you that in this club, it's exactly the reverse . . .

The last time something like this happened to me I was given an Illuminated Address . . . when I got home I found they'd burnt my house down. Not that I'm suggesting that anything like that would happen here, mind you . . . everyone has been so kind and friendly to me – in fact when I first arrived I bumped into an old pal of mine from way back. 'Hello,' I said to him, 'how are you, Vanessa?' Well, we always called him that because he had a terrible childhood – he was dragged up. He said, 'I've just got married.' I said, 'That's good.' He said, 'It's not so good, the wife's very ugly.' I said, 'That's bad.' He said, 'It's not so bad, she's very rich.' I said, 'That's good.' He said, 'It's not so good, she's very mean.' I said, 'That's bad.' He said, 'It's not so bad. We live in a big house in the country.' I said, 'That's good.' He said, 'It's not so good. Last week it burnt down.' I said, 'That's bad,' He said, 'It's not so bad – she was in it.'

So I took him behind the bar, 'cos he was a bit upset – weren't you, Clem.[3] I went up to Bill behind the bar [4] and I thought I'd have a bit of fun, 'cos he looks the cheery sort, doesn't he? . . . strewth [5] . . . so I said, 'Do you serve Yorkshiremen?' He said, 'Of course' in his usual forthright manner, so I said, 'Right – give us a pint of Special and two Yorkshiremen for my crocodile!' [6]

But I must tell you, just to prove what I said about people being friendly to me here, when I went around looking for somewhere to stay the night I wasn't having much luck finding a room. Eventually I knocked on the door of this little boarding house, quite near here, as it happens. Only a stone's throw away – you can't miss it – all the windows are broken . . . the landlady opened a window in answer to my ring and said, 'What ya want?' Very genteel class of woman she was. I said, 'Well, I'd like to stop here for the night.' She said, 'All right – so stop there!' and slammed the window.

But when we got that sorted out and she gave me a lovely room with a superb view right out over the Wanstead Sewage Farm.[7] It's got hot and cold running . . . I don't know what they are but it makes you go hot and cold to hear 'em running . . . The family all seem very nice. The landlady told me that her old grandfather – he lives with them – he's a very active member of the (*local*) Darby and Joan club. She told me she doesn't know what he does there but after only two weeks he'd got three notches on his walking-stick . . .

You certainly look after your old folks in this borough, don't you? She told me that old grandad is a very keen member of the Chigwell Halt (*or local*) Over Sixties Nudist Leapfrog Team. One day he was backing up to take a run over his regular partner when the door opened behind him and in came the lady with the club tea-pot . . . well, you can imagine . . . ! Impaled is probably the word . . . it was a very distressing occasion for everyone there . . . especially for those who were waiting for a cup of tea . . . Anyway, eventually the tea-lady and one of the staff prised grandad off the spout . . . he was in such a state! Well, you can imagine, can't you? 'Oh, I'm ruined!' he yelled, 'I'm full of hot tea! What's going to happen to me? What's going to happen?' And the tea-lady bent down and said, 'You're going on a long journey . . .'[8]

On my way here I saw this chap – I couldn't believe my eyes! He was wearing a kilt – upside-down! Upside-down! I said to him, 'Please excuse me, but I'm a stranger in town – why have you got that kilt on upside-down?' He said, 'Well, I'm going to a fancy-dress ball.' I said, 'What as?' He said, 'A shuttlecock . . .' I couldn't understand what he meant . . . I think he must have been from (*local*).

My mother told me that one . . . but my wife would have loved to have been here tonight – yes, I am married, ladies, sorry about that – my wife would have liked so much to be here, but she's been refused bail. Mind you, she hates being away from home. The other weekend I was very late back, duet to points failure or something on the railway track. She was furious! 'You should have been here hours ago,' she said. 'Darling,' I said – I always call her that because I *keep* forgetting her name – 'Darling,' I said, 'I couldn't help it. The train was delayed.' She said, 'look at the time. Four o'clock in the morning – and we've had a burglar in the house.' I said, 'Oh dear – did he get anything?' She said, 'Yes – I thought it was you . . . !'

But I shouldn't complain, really, because she's a lovely girl – she's got everything a man could desire . . . big – biceps and a black bushy beard . . . she comes from around here, as it happens . . . from Stepney (*or local rough district*), it's a beautiful spot, I'm told, where all the big knobs hang out. Some of you remember my wife, perhaps. She used to be known as the Toast of Tooley Street [9] (*or local*) although I believe that the last Duke to drink champagne from her

121

slipper succumbed shortly afterwards to a bad attack of athlete's gullet . . .

I must thank you for all those kind words you said about me, Mr Chairman – you read my handwriting beautifully. Thank you so much for having me, and for those who haven't – please be patient.

Suggested Headings

May you live as long.

No pro would turn down chance of free meal.

Nearly late – changing wheel/man starts to take battery.

All enjoy dinner?

Strange custom – after dinner speaking/animals sleep.

Thanks to committee. Usually only half committee do work.

Illuminated Address.

Friend in bar. Good and Bad Routine.

Bill behind bar. Serve Yorkshiremen?

Looked for room. Boarding house stone's throw away.

'I want to stop here for the night.'

Superb view over Wanstead Sewage Farm.

Hot and Cold Running.

Grandad. Darby and Joan. Three notches on stick. Chigwell Halt. Over 60's Nudist Leapfrog Team. Impaled on tea-pot.

Man in kilt upside down/shuttlecock.

Wife refused bail.

Late home. Burglar. 'I thought it was you!'

Has everything a man could desire.

Comes from Stepney.

Toast of Tooley Street/last Duke.

Thanks for reading my handwriting.

Thanks for having me.

Notes

As in all the suggested headings for all the speeches in this book, I have written out local place names and persons' names in full. If you are a stranger to the locality and/or the people, don't rely on your memory because in the stress of the moment it will fly completely from your consciousness.

1. 'Groovy' can be replaced by some similiar slightly out-of-date trendy adjective.
2. The 'pro' will of course be altered to fit your own particular capacity.
3. 'Clem' will be the club butt. Make sure he hasn't recently been widowed. It is best if you refer to a middle-aged or elderly bachelor for this story.
4. 'Bill' will be the barman or steward most likely to be popular. If he is habitually cheery you can alter this and say, 'I thought I'd try and cheer him up because he's always so down in the dumps, isn't he . . . ? Worried about his whippets or something . . .' The reference to whippets will go down very well if he is known to be devoted to greyhounds – alter to suit.
6. The reference to Yorkshiremen only makes sense if Bill is a Yorkshireman and desperately proud of it. Again, as in so many of these speeches, alter to suit.
7. Wanstead Sewage Farm – substitute any local eyesore.
8. On 'You're going on a long journey' you must bend down and look sideways.
9. 'Tooley Street' – the local equivalent should be a street in a notoriously rough district which begins with the letter T.

All the gags about the landlady and the couple in the street and the wife coming from 'this' area are standard patter and should be adjusted accordingly. Obviously I cannot give the definitive speech for this particular occasion because circumstances alter cases, but in the foregoing you should find a framework on which to build a suitable reply. And as I have said before, do your best to get a sight of the proposer's speech beforehand, even if you have to ask him to post a copy to you! Check local references on a map

– the AA Illustrated Guide To Britain is especially valuable for this, I have found. Asking locals is rarely productive, oddly enough; it is much better to glim over a street-map yourself and then test the caretaker or doorman or cloakroom attendant for reactions.

20

House Warming: Proposal

Ladies and gentlemen, your attention please. For those of you who don't know me, my name is Jane Fonda [1] . . . I have been *deputed* . . . I rather enjoyed that . . . *deputed* to give utterance to a few remarks appropriate to the occasion. So – a Happy Christmas to you all, and a prosper – what? House-warming? . . . oh . . . well. I don't know about you but whatever this party's for I'm having a rip-roaring time. Every time I rip some girl roars,

But isn't this a great house? It'll be really lovely when it's finished. [2] I'm not sure about that suite, though. I wonder who shot the traffic warden? [3] Actually, I happen to know that Christine was trying to get a new suite to match the colour of her eyes, but they told her in (*local store*) they didn't do bloodshot sofas. That wall's going to have an old master on it . . . and that one an old mistress . . . but the general decor throughout the house [4] is very . . . isn't it? It was done by Ashton's [5] . . .

The carpet's nice, isn't it? Do you know what you get if you cross a carpet with an elephant? A big pile in your sitting-room . . .

But did you ever see their old place . . . ? (*make bad smell face*) Mind you, I'm not surprised. They used to keep a goat in the spare room. A goat! I said to Dick one day, 'What about the smell?' He said, 'Oh, the goat'll have to get used to it like the rest of us . . .'

It's a shame they didn't take the opportunity to buy a new gas stove, though. Have you seen that old one? It's bow-legged . . . Christine always did have a heavy hand with the pastry. Mind you, their old kitchen was a bit of a mess. Especially after Christine drove their car smack into the middle of it. Dick came rushing in from the front and there she was, still at the wheel. Dick said, 'How did you get there?' She said, 'I just turned left at the dustbins . . .'

Talking of accidents in the home, a friend of mine had this au pair girl staying with them. She was from Lapland actually – not much good around the house, really, but a knock-out at milking reindeer. Anyway, this friend of mine had a full-sized statue of a Greek discus-thrower in his sitting-room, and being Greek it was a bit under-dressed. Starkers, in fact. So thus au pair is trying her little hand at dusting and – wait for it – she accidentally knocked a bit of the statue off. She must have had lightning reactions, because she managed to catch it [6] . . . and as it hadn't broken she was able to stick it back on. But when my pal's wife came in from the shops, the first thing she noticed was the join, so she called the girl in and said, 'What's been going on here then?' The girl burst into tears and told her what had happened and said, 'I hoped no-one would notice.' My pal's wife said, 'Well, they might not have done, but you've stuck it back on upside-down.' 'Have I?' said the girl, 'I've only ever seen them like that . . .' [7]

But this is a nice neighbourhood, isn't it? Not like where Christine and Dick used to live. Dick told me he came home once and said to Chris that he'd heard the milkman there had made love to every woman in the street [8] except one. And Chris said, 'I'll bet it's that stuck-up cow at number forty-three . . .' I've always had a sentimental affection for this part of the world, as it happens. My first grand passion came from here – she was a gorgeous girl and I was nuts about her. I told her I'd follow her to the ends of the earth. I would have done too, but she moved to Sunderland (*or local*) . . .

The move in wasn't without its problems, though. Moving is always a terrible caper, isn't it? Dick told me he saw one of the removal men struggling up the stairs with their big wardrobe all on his own. Dick said, 'Why don't you get your mate to help you?' He said, 'Oh, he's inside carrying the clothes . . .' The next-door neighbours are a bit strange here, as well. Dick met the husband in the street this morning carrying their front door under his arm, so Dick said, 'What are you carrying that around for?' He said, 'I've lost my key.' Dick, with that ready wit which we all know and fear, said, 'So how will you get in then?' And the neighbour said, 'I've left a window open . . .'

I was privileged to be given a preview of the house shortly after Dick and Christine moved in. Dick proudly showed me round this lovely big room and the marvellous kitchen – but as we were leaving the kitchen he looked out of the window and shouted 'Green side up!' We went upstairs and had a look at the bedrooms – have you seen the mirrors all over the ceiling? – and again Dick looked out of the window of the back bedroom and shouted 'Green side up!' We had a look at the bathroom – smashing! Beautiful tiles, low-flush, footbath – and yet again he looked out of the window and shouted 'Green side up!' I couldn't restrain my curiosity any longer, so I said, 'Look, Dick, what is this "green side up" routine that you keep shouting?' He said, 'Oh, that's the garden – I've got two Irishmen laying the lawn . . .'

But I'm sure, Christine and Dick, you are going to be very happy in your new home, and I for one will be happy to come round and tread crisps into the Axminster any old time. Here's to you and number sixteen! [9]

Suggested Headings

Jane Fonda.
Deputed. Happy Xmas.
Rip-roaring time.
Great house when it's finished.
Suite? Who shot traffic warden?
Colour of her eyes / bloodshot sofas.
Old master / mistress.
Decor by Ashton's.
Carpet / elephant. Big pile.
Old place: goat in spare room.
Why no new gas stove? Old one bow-legged.
Christine parked in kitchen.
Au pair knocked piece off statue. 'I've only ever seen them like that'.

Nice neighbourhood here. Old place: milkman made love to every woman except one.

Used to have girl locally. Said I'd follow her to the ends of the earth.

Moving a horrible caper. Moving man carrying heavy wardrobe on his own.

New neighbour with front door under his arm.

Preview of house: 'green side up' two Irishmen laying the lawn.

I'll be happy to tread crisps into your Axminster any time.

Notes

If the new home is a flat, the following jokes might be appropriate;

These high-rise flats have their problems. A couple I know moved into one and the husband said to his wife, 'Now you must keep this place nice and clean.' The following morning she went out and wasn't seen for a week. When she finally came in her husband said, 'Where have you been?' She said, 'I was doing the steps.'

Then there was the chap who had a dog – he was also in a high-rise block, and the dog kept getting caught short and doing its business on the stairs. So the chap decided to train it, and every time the dog misbehaved he'd rub its nose in it and throw it down the stairs. This went on for a month, sometimes two and three times a day. Now when the chap takes the dog out it does its business on the stairs, rubs its nose in it and chucks itself over the bannisters . . .

1. Or any wildly inappropriate, fashionably glamorous name. If you are fashionable and glamorous already, announce yourself as some current unpopular politician and follow up the boos and hisses by saying, 'I thought I'd give you the bad news first . . .'
2. Look around as you say this line and let your smile change momentarily to one of pitying disgust.

3. Obviously this must be altered to suit any especially startling feature of the room – drapes, wall-paper, light fitments, carpet – in which you are speaking.
4. Or 'in this room.' After the word 'very' you will appear to search for a suitable adjective but fail.
5. 'Ashton's' will be the local funeral directors. If there is no well-known local firm the gag goes just as well by spelling it out, i.e., 'It was done by Messrs. Ashton & Co, High Class Funeral Directors, of High Street and Station Parade.'
6. Mime catching the object as you speak this line.
7. You can attempt an accent for the au pair girl. I have made her a Laplander just for the sake of the reindeer gag and to demonstrate how useless she was around the house and therefore liable to make blunders. But the au pair can just as easily come from some unsalubrious town nearby.
8. 'Street' will naturally be changed to block or square or estate as appropriate.
9. Or the name of the house.

References can also be made to the vast expanse of the new home ('I won't say how much it is but have you noticed Dick's rolling his own these days?') and to the reactions of any pets or children ('Rover's already on friendly terms with all the lamp posts in the street.' 'They bought a new watchdog. He only watches television.' 'Ivor's made friends with the boy next door. He's named after his father, Ivor told me. They call him Dad.')

21

House Warming: Reply

Ladies and gentlemen. That's the only bit I've prepared – the rest of my speech is all downhill. A home has been described as a place to go to when all the other joints are closed, but I am sure you will appreciate that with such a house I couldn't afford any other joints . . . But no, this is so much better than our old house. For a start, back in (*wherever*) the walls were so thin you could hear the next door neighbours changing their minds . . . and if any of you ever met the Ropers you'll appreciate what a stomach-churning experience that could be . . .

By the way, Harry,[1] this is a house-warming party not a Fancy Dress . . . what have you come as – Titania[2] . . . ? We have refreshments laid on for you all in the breakfast room. Christine has made Scotch broth just the way I like it . . . with real Scotch. We were going to have tongue sandwiches but I thought some of you might not like anything that had been in an animal's mouth, so there will be egg sandwiches instead . . .

Then after you've eaten it will be cabaret time. One or two disappointments there, I'm afraid. I had wanted The Dance of the Three Virgins . . . but unfortunately they've broken their contract. Then we were to have had that wonderfully exciting knife-throwing act, Los Fundadores and Doris, but Doris is still in hospital . . . Anyway, we do have for you the famous fire-eater, Tongueless Thomas[3] . . .

There are some old family pieces scattered around the house – some were left to me by my grandfather. Well, really, all he left was a cuckoo clock so it didn't take long to wind up his estate. I must buy a better brand of cracker next Christmas . . . That blank wall here is reserved for a portrait of Christine. I wanted something special so when I originally commissioned the artist I said, 'Can you paint my wife in the nude?' He said, 'Certainly – as long as I can keep my socks on, I must have somewhere to put the brushes...'

Our furniture comes from F-Plan ... it came before G-Plan ... yes, it's F in this house from top to bottom ... Mind you, we're very conveniently situated here – conveniences at each end of the street ... we're very handy for the Park, the Shops, the Library and the Magistrates' Court ... the Cricket Club is quite close, too, and for any of you interested in cricket, by the way, I have a marvellous old well-oiled bat upstairs which you can see, provided you don't wake her up ... There's quite a good pub nearby also, which I discovered quite by chance, you understand ... Christine isn't so keen on me going there, though. The other night I stagg – came back and she said, 'I know why you keep going to that pub. It's that tarty barmaid, isn't it? Well, what's she got that I haven't got?' I said: 'Some clean glasses and a good pair of pumps!' Well, you must be honest [4] ...

I know this is a very select neighbourhood and we're so pleased to be here, but I must confess I was a little dismayed when I read in the Church Times that fifty per cent of the wives in (local) were unfaithful to their husbands. Did you know that? Yes, well it seems, according to the Church Times, that the Archbishop of Canterbury wrote letters to the faithful fifty per cent, to congratulate them and encourage them. And do you know what he said ... ? (this directed to the wife of one of your new neighbours) ... why – didn't you get one?

But it's marvellous of you all to come to this housewarming. Tomorrow we're having a house-clearing-up – anyone like to come to that ... ? Thanks again, and in the words of the Bard: 'We'll teach you to drink deep 'ere you depart.' Skol!

Suggested Headings

Ladies and gents – only bit prepared.
Home. Place to go to when all the other joints are closed.

Back in (*previous*) walls so thin.

Harry. Not a Fancy Dress party.

Scotch broth.

Tongue sandwiches/egg sandwiches.

Cabaret disappointments. Dance of the Three Virgins.

Knife-throwing act. Los Fundadores and Doris.

Fire eater. Tongueless Thomas.

Grandfather left cuckoo clock/wind up estate.

Commissioned portrait of Christine. Ask artist whether he could paint her in the nude.

Furniture from F-Plan.

Conveniently situated/convenience.

Park – Shops – Library – Magistrates' Court.

Cricket Club. Old and well-oiled bat upstairs.

Pub. What has that barmaid got that I haven't.

50% of wives round here are unfaithful to so AB of C wrote to the others.

Tomorrow a house-clearing-up.

'We'll teach you to drink deep 'ere you depart'.

Notes

1. Harry will be a 'character', rather outrageously dressed and delighted to have attention drawn to him.
2. Titania was the fairy queen – a reference which may or may not be appropriate. Your choice of epithet should be appropriate both to the costume and the wearer.
3. This list of cabaret artistes can be prolonged indefinitely as required, but generally speaking three is enough.
4. If you want this gag to be less offensively directed towards your wife, just say: 'Christine isn't keen on me going there, though, I think it's that barmaid ... but she really does possess a marvellous pair of pumps. Anyway, she's not there any more – the landlord gave her the push. She kept dipping in the till ...'

If you have no television, you can say: 'We've given up television. Well, it just breeds violence – we used to have one and every time I switched it on Christine used to thump me.'

If you are in a high-rise block, you can say: 'We're better off than the next block – the lifts are at a standstill there, they tell me. The lifts stay where they are and the flats go up and down.'

The following may be of possible use:

Isn't that a marvellous old picture? It's a family heirloom, you know . . . it was handed down to me by my father . . . he was still on the ladder when the police arrived . . .

22

Ladies' Night: Proposal

'A woman is only a woman, but a good cigar is a smoke' – Kipling's words, not mine, and if you've never liked Kipling, ladies, perhaps that's because you have never kippled with the right person. I just give that celebrated quotation to show that that kind of jocularly offensive remark is nowadays just as unacceptable as the usual gushing stream of smug and fatuous gallantries about a woman's hair or face or figure or sensuality, as though she were a cross between an oriental concubine and a brood mare.

The situation now is fraught with pitfalls for the unwary if well-meaning speaker – for instance, just to mention Women's Lib, even approvingly, is to invite the wrath of a monstrous regiment of prickly feminists, so to you ladies here tonight, I promise I will not patronize you by making any of those boring jokes about the battle of the sexes, equality, male chauvinism, feminine wiles, and the customary demeaning malarkey. No, I will just say to you – welcome, and did you turn off the gas?

But I can see from here that you are truly a well-liberated set of females – not a bra in sight. Yes, we're really going to have a swinging time of it tonight – no! . . . But old habits die hard, and when on my way here tonight in the bus . . . all I could afford – my mother-in-law drinks the rest of it away . . . she was thrown out of the Mafia for cruelty – a young girl asked for my seat because she was expecting. I had no hesitation in acceding to her request. As I got up I said, 'Excuse me, but you don't look very . . . er . . . how long has it been, then?' To which she replied, 'Only half an hour, but doesn't it make your back ache . . . ?'

But you see, mediaeval canonists debated very earnestly whether women were entirely human, whether they possessed souls. I say, however, scratch the surface of any woman and she'll say, 'Just a *teeny* bit lower . . .'[1]

There again, a woman with a past attracts men who hope history will repeat itself . . . Notice I said a 'woman' with a past and not a lady, because despite these emancipated times . . . are you emancipated, dear?[2] . . . you want to try bile beans . . . marvellous! . . . where was I? Oh, yes . . . are you 'ladies'? Or are you just 'women'? The word 'gentleman' has very specific connotations, doesn't it? Politeness, consideration, integrity, fair play and all that rubbi – all that . . . but 'lady' isn't quite the same, is it? Originally the word came from the Anglo-Saxon – and you know what they were like . . . strewth! . . . meaning Bread-Kneader. You may think things haven't changed all that much[3] . . . no, that's kneader with a K – the I is moist as in onion[4] . . . but I think a good modern definition of a lady is a woman who can pull up a shoulder strap without looking like a small boy scooping his cap out of a puddle[5] . . .

Of course, I've been interested in women's clothes for the past twenty years . . . on and off . . . I think a good instance of the change in attitudes between the sexes was afforded earlier this evening on that same bus I was telling you about. After that stimulating conversation with the pregnant young . . . person . . . I got a seat upstairs and found myself sitting by this courting couple, locked in passionate embrace. Do you know, the boy kissed the girl all the way from the top of Highgate Hill (*or local*) . . . to the bottom of Hampstead Road (*or local*) . . . without coming up for air! Eventually they pulled apart and sat gazing into each other's eyes . . . panting. Then the girl, in tones that were shy but charged with an ardent intensity, said to her swain, 'Hey, Englebert . . . got any ciggies?'[6] The lad was so upset – you could tell. The mood was shattered, the spell broken. He said, 'Have I got –? Ain't you got no emotions, no finer feelings?' She said, 'I dunno, but I know I ain't got any ciggies . . .'[7]

But it isn't fair, is it? We still think of a woman who kicks over the traces as being so much more depraved than a man. A woman who drinks and fights and gambles and fornicates – not you, mother, siddown[8] – is looked upon

135

with the utmost disdain, whereas the man who indulges himself to excess excites a degree of rueful admiration. I suppose most men fancy themselves now and then as a roué or a Casanova, but ladies, there's no percentage in being a slut, or worse, a slag.

Mind you, there was one young girl, about to go off on holiday on her own, was warned by her mother not to accede to temptation – 'Or I shall worry myself silly,' said the mother. So on holiday this girl met a very charming and attractive chap; she had a few drinks, dinner and dancing and he invited her back to his hotel room. But she thought, 'No – my mother would worry.' The next day she saw more of him – again they went swimming and drinking and wining and dining and again he asked her back to his hotel room, but again she thought, 'No – my mother would worry.' But the third day, after a wonderful time together all day long, full of the romance of the moonlight and warm Mediterranean breezes, not to mention Gordon's, when yet again he asked her to go back to his hotel room, she thought, 'Oh, what the hell – let *his* mother worry . . .'

Anyway, women have been likened to the continents. From the age of 20 to 30 they are like the United States – young and fresh but green and over-eager. From 30 to 45 they are like Africa – mysterious and steamily mature. From 45 to 60 they are like Europe, battered, but ripely experienced and still game. From 60 onwards they are like Australia – everyone knows where it is but who the hell wants to go there? On which courteous and chivalrous note I will ask all the gentlemen to rise, if you'll pardon the expression, and charge their glasses for the toast: To our wives and sweethearts – may they never meet! [9]

Suggested Headings

A woman is only a woman.
Kipling/kippled.
That kind of jocularly offensive remark nowadays unacceptable.
Pitfalls for unwary if well-meaning speaker. Women's Lib.

No mention of battle of the sexes, equality, male chauvinism, feminine wiles etc. Welcome – and did you turn off the gas?

Not a bra in sight – swinging time tonight.

On bus coming here (ma-in-law thrown out of Mafia for cruelty).

Pregnant girl asked for my seat.

Mediaeval canonists debated whether women had souls.

Scratch the surface of any woman.

Woman with past attracts men who hope history will repeat itself.

Woman – not lady – are you emancipated? Bile beans.

Gentlemen – politeness, consideration, integrity, fair play.

Lady: Anglo-Saxon meaning Bread-Kneader.

Modern definition: Lady is a woman who can pull up a shoulder-strap without etc.

Interested in women's clothes for the past 20 years.

Back on bus. Couple kissing from top of (*local*) to bottom of (*local*). Girl: 'got any ciggies?'

Woman who kicks over traces so much worse than a man. 'Not you mother, siddown.'

Most men fancy themselves as roué or Casanova – no percentage in being slut or slag.

Young girl on holiday alone for the first time. 'Let his mother worry'.

20–30 like United States: young and fresh but green and over-eager.

30–45 like Africa: mysterious and steamily mature.

45–60 like Europe: battered but ripely experienced and still game.

Over 60 like Australia: everyone knows where but who wants to go.

Rise gents (if you'll pardon the expression) charge glasses for the toast: to wives and sweethearts – may they never meet!

Notes

1. The word 'teeny' should be dragged out and accompanied by a suitable arching of the back and a glazed expression on the face.

2. This can be perhaps addressed to someone by name, provided you are sure that the lady will not object later (some people smile while burning up inside, and you will wonder for years why you didn't get that promotion . . .) and that the name will mean something to the majority of those present.

3. 'And you may think . . . that much' is a throwaway, an aside.

4. 'The I is moist' is just a silly nonsensical line which always gets a surprisingly good reaction, so if you are using this section I would advise you to leave it in. Even if people don't quite understand it, the remark sounds witty and they will laugh.

5. Obviously you make make the appropriate bending movement on the tag.

6. 'Englebert' should be altered to the latest rock superstar – or to the first name or nickname of any suitable personality in the room.

7. This type of joke is three times as funny if delivered in the local accent.

8. If your mother is well-known and is patently not present, then obviously you must change this to 'Not you, Nola, siddown' or whatever. There are two slightly less direct alternatives, (a) to cut the 'siddown' line entirely and to say after the word 'disdain', 'Isn't she, Nola . . .?' or, (b) at the same point – after the word 'disdain' – to say 'Oh, I dunno, though – Eric's perked up all of a sudden . . .' A third possibility is to pause after the word 'disdain' and say bluntly, 'Isn't she, Nola?' But you must be very sure of your victim and your audience before working the gag that way.

9. This toast is quite well known and you may well find some know-alls anticipating you – if this happens: *don't say the tag!* Which makes them look gauche and you're

in the clear. If you have done a few 'but seriously' sentences prior to the toast it is probably better not to attempt a joke at all, but just to say quite simply, 'gentlemen, will you charge your glasses and be upstanding and drink the health of – the ladies!

23

Ladies' Night: Reply

Thank you, Mr Chairman . . . know any jokes? . . . and to all you gentlemen, our thanks for graciously permitting us to join you tonight. It's a big concession because I know how busy you boys always are, and so I'd like you to know we are properly grateful . . . (*aside*) did I say it right, George? [1] . . .

I won't keep you long – Ivy Benson's rejects are all set to crack a few quavers for dancing. Besides, I've been coming to these bunfights for a good few years now and if there's one thing I've learned it is that the success of the evening is in direct proportion to the brevity of the speeches . . . especially when I'm making one . . . So I'll finish by saying, girls, don't worry too much about the men in your life . . . it's the life in your men that counts . . . but whatever you think of the boys, always remember:

> *We owe a lot to Father,*
> *Let no-one here say nay.*
> *Without him there just wouldn't be,*
> *A thing called Mother's Day.*

Thanks again, fellas. 'Locheim!' [2]

Suggested Headings

Know any jokes?
Thanks for permitting us to join you/big concession/did I say it right?
Ivy Benson's rejects.
Success of the evening in direct proportion to brevity of speeches.
Don't worry about men in your life. Life in your men.
We owe a lot to Father,

Let no-one here say nay.
Without him there just wouldn't be
A thing called Mother's Day.

Notes

Unless you are a very experienced speaker or a professional comedienne (in which case you won't be needing any help from me) I think the above is all you need. Try to find out a day or two beforehand what the proposer intends saying – you might be able to hang a telling point on one of his remarks. If this is not possible, have a pencil handy during his speech so that you can jot down any comments which may occur to you – in this respect the replying speaker has the advantage.

1. 'George' will be your husband or some senior official of the organization sitting by your side.
2. Say this last line quickly and sit down during the buzz of appreciation which will follow the verse.

Two possible aphorisms:

A gentleman is one who never hurts anyone's feelings unintentionally, and a lady is one who never shows her underwear unintentionally.

A lady is a woman who makes a man behave like a gentleman.

If suiting the occasion, the following story might be used:

A widow was receiving a friend's condolences on her recent loss. 'I didn't know your husband all that well,' said the friend, 'but I'm told he was ever such a nice person.' 'Yes, he was,' sniffed the bereaved. 'Mind you – I didn't know him all that well either. He was secretary of (*give the name of the group you are addressing*) ...'

If you find to your dismay that you are to follow a particularly scintillating speech, cut your losses and use the cop-out given on page 16. If however the content makes this inappropriate, just say, 'What a wonderful speech –

worth every penny. I've had to get mine out of the house-keeping . . . and you all know how heavy my Jack is on groceries . . .' and carry on as planned. This will get you so much sympathy than the rest of your speech will do very well.

24

The Law

It was a Jewish friend of mine who pointed out to me that the rule of law in all civilized countries was founded upon the Ten Commandments. 'There, you see,' he said, 'even your basic moral precepts you stole from us.' 'That's true,' I said, 'but you can't say we've kept them . . .'

I've always thought that when the Lord gave the tablets to Moses on Mount Sinai He should have added a rider: only six to be attempted.[1]

But you must at all times have the courage of your convictions – no matter how long your record, walk tall . . . like my Dad, bless him. He nearly died young from a nasty fall . . . might have hurt himself if he hadn't had a rope round his neck . . .

I was brought up in Brighton – nothing serious, a misunderstanding really. I'd had a jugful and there were these two French au pair girls on the open-top bus . . . they were wearing open-top dresses and one thing led to another . . . ah me! Sic transit gloria mundi . . . which roughly translated means, 'Gloria should be all right by Monday . . .' (*cross your fingers and look fervently upwards*)

Mind you, this Latin business is one of the things lawyers use to maintain the mystique of their profession. There was one famous occasion when a chap was up on a charge of assaulting a young girl and at one point in the trial the judge said he'd like to hear the rest of the evidence in camera, and ordered for the court to be cleared. 'What's this in camera bit, then?' asked the defendant. 'Never mind about that,' said the judge. 'I know what it means, your counsel knows what it means, and the jury knows what it means. Carry on with your evidence.' So the defendant said, 'Well, this bird and me was wandering across (*local*) – beautiful spot at this time of year – and I kissed her, right in the middle of the common. Anyway, she fainted! Spark out on the deck! So it was all dark, no-one about, so I thought "Right – chance for a bit of how's-yer-father" –' The judge interrupted him and said, 'Wait a minute – what's "how's-yer-father"?' The defendant said, 'Well, I know what it means, my counsel knows what it means, the jury knows what it means – and if you'd been there with your ruddy camera you'd know what it means . . . !'

But there are all kinds of lawyers nowadays – some who know the law and some who know the judge . . . A neighbour of mine, a shrewd old cuss, he had a dispute with someone so he went along to his solicitor and came out with this long diatribe of grievances. After three hours he finally came to the end of the recital and said, 'Well – what do you think?' And his solicitor said 'You've got a very good case there, sir, I should institute proceedings if I were you.' 'Oh, no,' said the cunning old neighbour, 'I don't want to take any action – that was the other fellow's case I've just told you!'

The law is getting so complex, but the Law Society's protest against the continuing flood of new laws out of Westminster every year was met with the reply that every sentence of it was absolutely necessary; and as any lawyer can tell you 'necessity knows no laws . . .'

It's hard enough for the professional so it isn't surprising that the layman gets confused. One judge in a criminal trial was halfway through his summing up when he was outraged to see one of the jurymen sound asleep in the box. He indicated to the usher to wake the man up and then said furiously, 'How long have you been asleep?' 'I dunno,' said the juryman. 'How long have you been talking . . . ?' [2] As it happened, that jury gave a verdict of not guilty. The judge was furious. 'What?' he said, when the foreman made his announcement. 'Not guilty, my lord,' said the foreman again. 'Louder, louder!' said the indignant judge, 'I want the whole world to hear you!' . . .

This dilemma of personal opinion versus professional obligation was nicely resolved on one occasion by none other than Abraham Lincoln. He was a lawyer, and on one occasion appeared in two quite separate cases before the

144

same judge on the same day. Both cases involved a similar point of law, but in the morning Lincoln pleaded for the plaintiff and in the afternoon for the defendant – on each occasion with the utmost sincerity and forcefulness The morning case had been won, but half way through the afternoon's case the judge said, 'How come your change of attitude, Mr Lincoln?' To which Young Abe replied, 'This morning I may have been wrong, but this afternoon I know I am right.' [3]

And it is still unfortunately the case that there is one law for the rich and another for the very rich. One wealthy man up for murdering a business associate managed, through his minions, to have one of the jury bribed to persuade the other jurors to find not guilty of murder but guilty of the lesser charge of manslaughter. The accused was duly found guilty of manslaughter and sentenced to five years – a lot better than life. The corrupt juryman went to prison to visit him, and was thanked by the businessman. 'It wasn't easy,' said the ex-juryman, 'the others were all for acquittal . . . !'

The intricacies of the law are very daunting to the layman. I knew a woman whose husband died leaving quite a considerable estate, and the protracted and complex legalities involved in the granting of probate and the subsequent administrative details caused her to say to me, 'I sometimes almost wish Jack hadn't died . . . !'

I was walking along the Strand one fine summer's day when I saw a very distinguished Silk hurrying towards me. I stopped him and said, 'Excuse me, can you tell me where the Law Courts are?' He was furious at being importuned in such an undignified way so he really wanted to put me in my place. 'You're standing right *outside* the Law Courts, man,' he said, 'are you blind or stupid or what?' 'Neither,' I said. 'I just wanted leading counsel's opinion for nothing . . .'

But counsel can be rather supercilious in court, you know. I remember one case where counsel was getting nowhere with a witness so finally in exasperation he said, 'Shall I put my questions in baby talk?' To which the

145

witness answered, 'All right, if it'll make it easy for you . . .'

You can't be too careful when you're an officer of the court, you know. One youth was in the dock for insulting behaviour and when his remarks were solemnly read out by a police constable even the case-hardened judge was taken aback. 'This is a dreadful way to behave,' he said. 'You went to a good school, your family is eminently respectable – where did you learn such language?' And the boy replied, 'I once caddied for you . . .'

Talking about the police reminds me – I saw in the local paper that police in (*local*) are looking for a tall, handsome man for assaulting women . . . I thought if the money was good I might apply [4] . . .

But I know the police make great efforts in their drive to make themselves more accepted by the young. At one school a prize was offered by the local station to the best action drawing of police officers apprehending criminals. This was won by a scruffy looking tyke from a notoriously anti-social family, but his drawing was undoubtedly the best so he was awarded first prize, which consisted of a ride in a patrol car, an inspection of the station control room and a visit to the cells. The boy was then taken to the canteen and given beans and pie and chips and lemonade and ice cream until it was coming out of his ears, and then, loaded down with drawing books and pencils and balloons he was taken home in a big shiny police car.

The next day he was asked to write an essay on his experiences, but his family background could not be gainsaid in one visit, and the essay consisted of a mere three words: 'Coppers is bastards'. The boy's teacher contacted the local station to tell them that their PR work had had no effect, so the local Super decided to pull out all the stops, and the following Saturday a patrol car whisked the boy up to London where he was taken round New Scotland Yard, he was shown the Black Museum, then taken on a police river-boat and up in a police helicopter. Eventually, at ten o'clock·at night, laden with presents and stuffed with chocs and ices, the boy was delivered to his door by a police car with flashing light and screaming siren. On the following Monday the boy was again asked to write an essay on his experiences. This time he was moved to write: Coppers is *crafty* bastards . . .

I'll keep you no longer because I want to get out there and put in some dancing cheek to cheek – in any direction – thank you.

Suggested Headings

Jewish friend: 10 Commandments.

Only six to be attempted.

Courage of convictions.

Dad – nasty fall / rope round his neck.

Brought up in Brighton / au pairs.

Sic transit gloria mundi.

In camera.

Neighbour in dispute consults solicitor – 'that was the other fellow's case'.

Flood of new laws from Westminster. Necessity knows no law.

Juryman asleep during summing up.

Judge outraged at not guilty verdict. Louder!

Lincoln. 'This morning I may have been wrong, but this afternoon I know I am right'.

One law for rich and another for very rich.

Businessman bribed juryman. 'The others were all for acquittal'.

Widow. 'I sometimes almost wish Jack hadn't died'.

Distinguished silk in Strand. 'Where are Law Courts?'

Counsel in court: 'Shall I put it in baby talk?'

Youth in dock to judge: 'I once caddied for you'.

Local police looking for tall handsome man for assaulting women.

Copper is (crafty) bastards.

Dancing cheek to cheek.

Notes

1. Obviously if you are Jewish yourself this opening story will have to be twisted, e.g. 'A certain friend of mine was

147

a very devout member of the Church of England, and I said to him one day, 'But you must realize that your whole social philosophy and rule of law is based upon an act of theft'. He said, 'What do you mean?' I said, 'The Ten Commandments – you stole them from the Jews'. He said, 'That's true . . . but you must admit we didn't keep them . . .'

2. As with many of the jokes illustrated in this book, this story will go very much better if told in the local dialect.

3. Contrariwise, I feel that this story is better told without attempting American accents, possibly because it has the feel of legend about it.

4. This story, which I admit is by no means news, is nevertheless always a winner, and can be helped along if the descriptions which you will read out from an actual copy of the local paper is totally at variance with your own appearance. The one exception to this is as follows: if you are lucky enough to be tall, dark and handsome, or similarly favoured, read the 'description' as such . . . believe me, it works.

The Law, as all professions, has its fund of stories true and apocryphal about the great names – Lord Birkenhead (F. E. Smith) being prominent in a calling noted for its quick wits. I have tried in the above to avoid the usual stories: if you are not a lawyer for goodness' sake take advice on your final draft – even if you have to pay a fee . . . Never impugn a lawyer's honesty or competence, even in fun, for they are touchier about their reputations than most. And not without reason, I suppose. For this reason I would advise, in this instance, that you do *not* personalize the jokes as I have so often recommended in previous pages.

Mae West's famous remark to a judge who warned her that she was showing contempt for his court – 'Sorry, Judge. I'll try to hide it' – might be useful. The following story is sometimes told about a bookmaker, and it goes like this: Two burglars raided a house, one climbing up a drainpipe to the first floor and the other staying below to keep guard. The first burglar returned to his colleague very quickly and said, 'Come on, let's get out of here'. 'Why?' said the other. 'Didn't you get anything?' 'Nah,' said the first, 'it's a ruddy lawyer's place.' 'Oh,' said the second, '... well, did you *lose* anything...?'

Also of possible use is the story of the juryman who asked to be excused service, and when asked his reasons by the judge replied that his wife was expecting a conception. To which the judge replied, 'I think you mean that she is expecting a confinement, but whichever it is I certainly agree that you must be there. You are excused'.

25

Medicine

Ladies and gentlemen, what an honour and a pleasure it is
to be dirtying a plate in the midst of so many eminent and
companionable members of the medical profession.[1] Actually, I've got this pain . . . (*indicate lumbar region*) . . . no!
I really did get out of a sick bed to come here – my girl-
friend's got 'flu . . . (*Pick up your neighbour's glass*) Is that
a drink or a sample . . . ? [2]

But what nice people here – I met a chap in the bar just
before dinner, and we got chatting. I said, 'Are you a
doctor?' He said, 'Yes, I'm a naval surgeon'. I thought,
'Well, I've heard of specialization but this is ridiculous . . .'

I've a lot to thank the profession for though. For a long
time, when I was a small boy, I used to think I was a dog!
. . . yes, a dog . . . I'm all right now though – feel my nose [3]
. . . But as it happens only this morning I woke up feeling
a little dicky – no, I was feeling a little hoarse . . . well, I'm
under canvas at the moment in (*local*) fields . . . Anyway, I
went to the surgery, rang the bell and this very dolly young
receptionist answered, so I said (*in a whisper*) 'Is the doctor
here?' She said, (*also in a whisper*) 'No – come in!'

Anyway, he arrived eventually, felt my pulse and said,
'Either you're dead or my watch has stopped . . . !' (*Laugh
heartily then say pathetically*): That was my best joke . . .
from now on it's all downhill . . . So the doctor said, 'What's
wrong?' I said, 'I've got long black hairs all down my back.'
So he gave me a ferret. But I'll say one thing for him – he
stopped me smoking: he tied a knot in my hookah . . . He
doesn't believe in all these patent medicines – he thinks
they're a drug on the market . . . in fact he told me that half
the modern drugs could be thrown out of the window . . .
except the birds might eat them.

My father didn't like him much, though – the old man
used to take everything he said with a grain of aspirin. My

Dad was a lazy old cuss – never did a stroke if he could avoid it. He went to this doctor once and asked for something to make him sweat. The doctor signed him off . . . I used to have a lot of trouble with my head – I had it on and off ever since I was a baby . . . You'd never believe it now but I'm still not quite right . . .

Mind you, our new GP's a clever man . . . he qualified in (*wherever*),[4] although I know academic distinctions aren't everything. He's got an MB, BCh, MD and PhD – so put 'em all together and what have you got? . . . MMMBCH-MMD-FFFD . . . Anyway, for any of you ladies on the Pill, the time is now half-past nine[5] . . . Which reminds me of the girl who went to her GP and said, 'I've got a very unusual complaint.' He said, 'Oh yes?' What's that then?'[6] 'Well, every time I sneeze I get an uncontrollable urge to make love . . .'[7] He said, 'Well, that *is* unusual – how long have you had this?' She said, 'Six months.' He said, 'Six months! What have you been taking for it?' She said, 'Snuff . . .'

But I did see a funny sight in his waiting-room. There were these three women with their daughters. He popped his head round the door, saw these women and flew into a great rage. 'It's no good you coming here,' he said, to the first, 'I've told you what your trouble is – you smoke too much. You must cut it out – you've even called your daughter after tobacco – you've called her Virginia. Pack it in.' Then he said to the second woman, 'I've told you not to waste my time as well. You drink too much, you must exercise some self-control. You've even called your daughter after an alcoholic drink – Sherry.' At which the third woman stood up and said, 'Come on Fanny, I haven't come here to be insulted . . .'[8]

Well, I'd better finish now – my injection is beginning to wear off. Thank you.

Suggested Headings

Honour to be dirtying a plate.
Got this pain.

Got out of sick bed.

Drink or a sample?

Naval surgeon.

Used to think I was a dog.

Woke up feeling a little dicky.

Little hoarse/under canvas in (*local*) fields.

Whisper to dolly receptionist.

'Either you're dead or my watch has stopped.' Best joke.

Long black hairs all down my back. Ferret.

Tied a knot in my hookah.

Patent medicines. Drugs on the market. Should be thrown out of the window.

Father took everything he said with a grain of aspirin.

Lazy. Asked for something to make him sweat.

Used to have trouble with my head.

Clever man, our GP. Qualified in (*wherever*).

MB BCh MD PhD.

Ladies on pill.

Every time I sneeze. Snuff.

Three women with daughters. Virginia, Sherry, Fanny.

Injection wearing off.

Notes

1. If you are a doctor yourself say 'In the midst of so many eminent and companionable colleagues . . .'
2. An alternative is to look up at the drink and say, 'I'm afraid it looks like diabetes, old man . . .' (You could even sip the drink first . . . !)
3. As you say, 'Feel my nose' take the hand of the person next to you and pull it towards your nose.
4. The place name given here can be a local area, or a town or even a country which suggests a low or non-existent standard of training.
5. Look at your watch as you say that.
6. 'What's that, then?' should be said in superior, world weary tones, as of a doctor who has seen it all and heard it all.
7. 'To make love' – this phrase can be sharpened, accord-

ing to how you gauge the mood of your audience, e.g. 'an uncontrollable urge for a man,' or 'an uncontrollable sexual urge', or even 'an uncontrollable urge to fornicate'.

8. The end of this line will be lost in a roar of laughter.

The following story may be thought suitable. I have frequently told it with great success, but not, I must admit, to a gathering of medicos.

An Army surgeon-general was making a surprise inspection of an Army hospital, and in one small ward he found three men, on their own. He said to the first, 'And what's your trouble, soldier?' The man said, 'Piles, sir!' 'I see,' said the general, 'and what treatment are you having?' 'Wire brush and paraffin, sir!' [1] 'Wire brush and paraffin, eh . . . I see [2] and what ambitions have you when you get out of here?' 'I'd like to fight in a lot of battles and win a chestful of medals and decorations like you, sir!' 'Very good . . . very good . . .' And the general passed to the second man. 'What brings you in here, soldier?' 'Piles, sir!' 'I see. And what treatment are you getting?' 'Wire brush and paraffin, sir!' 'Wire brush and . . . I see . . . and where do you see your career going when you get out of here?' 'I'd like to get a commission and become a senior officer like you, sir!' 'Very good . . . very good . . .' And the general passed to the third man. 'And what's your trouble, soldier?' (*In a hoarse whisper*) 'Laryngitis, sir!' [3] 'Laryn- . . . I see . . . and what treatment are you receiving?' 'Wire brush and paraffin, sir!' 'Wire br . . . I see . . . and what's your ambition, soldier?' 'To get the wire brush before them other two, sir!'

1. This last story must be characterized, with the general being of course very pukka and the three soldiers speaking in local dialects. Or the first two can be from elsewhere and just the third can speak in the local patois.
2. The general obviously does *not* see . . .
3. Give a long pause after 'laryngitis', to give your audience time to savour a possible outcome.

This is a very strong story, since the situation is novel and the tagline cannot possibly be guessed. It is also not perhaps a story to be told at a dinner, like the story of an old woman who complained to her GP about constant dreadful constipation, and when asked what she had been taking, replied, 'Just me knitting . . .'

The following joke underlies a common fear of doctors :
My grandfather didn't believe in doctors – he always treated himself from an old book of herbal remedies . . ; died of a printer's error.

If you are addressing a gathering of dentists, instead of the joke right at the beginning ('I've got this pain') you can pull your cheek open and point to some imaginary problem in your upper jaw. Jokes for dentists? There is the quite well-known one about the woman who was very scared of them, and as she sat in the chair she said, 'Oh, I don't know which is worse – having a filling or having a baby'. To which the dentist replied, 'Well, make up your mind before I adjust the chair . . .'

A lesser known continuation of this joke is as follows :
The dentist picked up a particularly fearsome instrument and the wretched patient blanched in terror. 'Don't worry,' said the dentist. 'It won't hurt.' 'But that – *thing* . . . !' 'I tell you I'm not going to hurt you,' said the dentist. 'But that *drill* . . . !' 'I'm not going to hurt you.' But the woman was still not convinced, so she grabbed the dentist by the . . . between his legs . . . and said, 'Now, we're not going to hurt each other, are we . . . ?'

26

Music

Ladies and gentlemen, good evening . . . GOOD EVEN-
ING! . . . thank you – sorry about that, but I'm a little
deaf. All that Wagner, you know . . . I agree with Mark
Twain's remark when he said that Wagner's music is better
than it sounds . . . Percy Grainger once said an interesting
thing . . . once . . . he defined music as a habit, like smoking
or spitting . . . or . . no, just smoking or spitting.

But music is all around us nowadays, whether we want
it or not. On my way here I passed a street busker, playing
Viennese waltzes on an old violin. I was quite struck by his
technique so I said to him, 'Do you always play by ear?' He
said, 'No, sometimes I play over there . . .'

But I am delighted to see so many people here tonight
with an interest in or a talent for music . . . because we want
some help shifting the piano – no! . . . I said to the Chairman, 'Did you go to the Marriage of Figaro in Glynde-
bourne last month?' And he said, 'No, but I sent a Greet-
ings Telegram.' I said, 'Surely you enjoy a night at the
opera.' He said, 'Oh yes – I'm mad about Harpo . . .' [1]

Of course some very great minds have had no appreciation of music – Walter Scott, Pitt, Peel, Tennyson – nor was
Dr. Johnson all that enamoured, and perhaps I may be
forgiven for repeating his comment: 'Of all noises I think
music the least disagreeable.' Let's see if he is right . . . we
have here several pros and not a few enthusiastic amateurs
– I'm talking about music, Chuck, siddown – so let us see
how tuneful we are . . . (*Tap glass with knife – or blow on
pitch-pipe*). That was a local A . . . sounded more like a
G-blunt to me . . . shall we try? . . . La-la-la-laaaa! (*Con-
duct singing at one table*) That's it! The lost chord! Let's
try over here – memememememeeee! . . . you-you-you-you-
youuuuu! . . . Sometimes I think Beethoven was lucky
being deaf . . . [2]

Did you like my voice? It was not only trained but shunted ... Of course, I came from a very musical family. My grandfather often played under Toscanini – used to give him a piggyback ... Grandma played the bass tuba and I understand that her embouchure had to be experienced to be believed. For many years she was in fact the only heavy brass in the entire Scunthorpe area (*or local*). I had a great-uncle who was known as the Hartlepools Heifetz (*or local*). At other times he was known as the Van Gogh of the violin, because he hadn't got much of an ear ... but he scraped a living ... someone in pain over there? ...

His sister, my great-aunt, played at the Albert Hall for years – in the Proms mostly. I once said to her, 'Sir Henry Wood?' She said, 'All the time if I'd let him.' Well, she was an oboist and you know what *they're* like ... My father could have been a great musician, but then he thought, 'Who wants to hear a grate?' So he studied and mastered the E flat Hoover ... not a lot of call for it, I know, but when you want one you really want one. He was a real pro, too ... on his way to a concert once he was involved in a nasty road accident, but managed to get to the concert hall where he played in three pieces. My mother was very keen on music although she had no formal training. She once went out and bought a music stool, but after three weeks she returned it to the shop saying, 'I've sat on this darn thing for three weeks now and haven't heard a note of music out of it yet!'

My brother was a very fine pianist – only recently he made his debut at the Combined (*local*) Spot-Welders, Commode Renovators and Midden Cleaners Association Hall ... playing Beethoven. Beethoven won. I remember when he was a lad he was taken for lessons to Artur Schnabel, who said that his lessons were ten guineas a time. My father said this was a little too much for the family fortunes, and could Mr Schnabel possibly see his way to a reduction? Schnabel said, 'I do give five guinea lessons ... but I don't recommend them ...'

My sister became a virtuoso on the slide trombone and

flit spray . . . her seventh position was the wonder of the LSO . . . 'B' team . . . I have another sister, who is now married. She used to play the banjo but now she just picks on her husband. As for myself, well, as a very young child I was known to play on the linoleum. In my teens my education was enriched by a girl student I met at the Royal College, she was a passionate music-lover . . . although she sometimes did it without . . .

First of all I tried the double-bass, but it kept making holes in my shoulder pad . . . then I tried the fiddle, but after three years found out I shouldn't have been trying to blow it. The classes at the Royal College were enormous in those days . . . besides which my gin kept sliding along the strings . . . so I took to the piano, although that was not without its problems because I devised my own technique. My teacher became furious and at one lesson she got so angry that she slammed the lid down, and broke three of my toes . . . But still the piano is my favourite instrument, and the piece I love to play most is Chopin's Nocturne in B major, opus 32, which, by the way, is the only one of Chopin's Nocturnes which has not been arranged by Liberace . . .

Anyway, I won't keep you because we having dancing this evening to that well known bachelor of music and father of six, Sledgehammer Charlie and his Over-Sextet – tonight they'll be playing as never before . . . in tune . . . so I'll just finish by telling you about a remarkable cat in my digs. My landlady knew that I was a musician – or at least a member of the Union, if you prefer – so she said, 'Would you like to see my Tiddles play?' I said, 'What – the cat?' She said, 'Yes!' I said, 'All right, ma, I'd love to see Tiddles play – always on the lookout for a good session man.' Anyway, this cat climbs up on a pile of cushions on the piano stool – and starts to play! Amazing! Fantastic – up and down the keyboard, scales, arpeggios, thirds – terrific. I said, 'That's amazing – he certainly plays well!' She said, 'Yes, he does, doesn't he?' I said. 'And that piece he's playing. That's very nice – did he write that himself?' She said, 'Yes, he did.' I said, 'that marvellous – have you had it orchestrated?' Well, you've never seen a cat move so fast in all your life . . . ! Thank you, folks.[3]

Suggested Headings

Little deaf. All that Wagner.

Wagner's music is better than it sounds.

Percy Grainger: Music a habit, like smoking or spitting.

Busker: Do you play by ear?

Chairman: Go to Marriage of Figaro? Enjoy a night at the Opera.

No appreciation of music – W. Scott, Pitt, Peel, Tennyson.

Dr Johnson: 'Of all noises I think music the least disagreeable.'

LA-LA-LA.

My voice trained / shunted.

Musical family.

Grandfather played under Toscanini. Piggyback.

Grandma played bass tuba. Embouchure. Only heavy brass in Scunthorpe.

Great-uncle Hartlepools Heifetz. Van Gogh of the violin. Scraped a living.

Great-aunt – Sir Henry Wood. Oboist.

Father great musician. E flat Hoover. Accident but played in three pieces.

Mother keen but no training. Music stool.

Brother pianist. Recent debut at Combined (*local*) Spot-Welders, Commode Renovators & Midden Cleaners Association Hall playing Beethoven.

Lessons from Artur Schnabel.

Sister virtuoso on slide trombone and flit spray 7th position.

Another sister now married used to play banjo.

Self. Used to play on linoleum.

Girl student music lover.

1st Double bass. Holes in shoulder pads.

2nd. Fiddle. After three years blowing it. Gin sliding.

3rd Piano. Own technique. Teacher slammed lid.

158

Favourite piece Chopin's Nocturne in B op. 32 not arranged by Liberace.

Dancing to B. Bus. and father of six (*name*) and his over-sextet/in tune.

Digs. Landlady's cat. Had it orchestrated?

Notes

1. The Chairman referred to should be some prominent member of the top table, known to all as someone to whom this story just conceivably might apply.
2. Getting the various tables or groups to sing a note can go on for quite some time, and you will probably find harmonies and variations creeping in, which you can deal with accordingly. There is the inevitable solo top-note, which can be squelched by your saying, 'Who's that treading on the cat?' or 'Who let that dog in here?' Or, 'You've been tippling on Sanderson's again . . .' (Sanderson's Throat Specific, a well-known emergency patent remedy for singers and actors).
3. The tag to the cat joke is a very big laugh so you can say 'Thank you, folks, or 'Take your partners, please' during it. Alternatively tell the band leader to take his cue from the tag so that the music can start straight away without any awkward pauses.

Musicians are extremely touchy about having their expertise impugned even in fun, which is why I have involved an imaginary family in all the 'incompetence' stories, but if you are sure that you will not offend it is always much stronger to name someone present. Sometimes a musician won't mind fun being made of his comparative lack of prowess on a second or third instrument, e.g. a man who plays 80 per cent of the time on sax will always admit to being rusty on the clarinet, and his flute technique will probably have almost vanished.

The following might be useful:

At half-past ten Piledriver Perce takes over as relief

pianist. It's such a relief when he stops.

Last week he was playing the Palladium, this week, with any luck, the piano.

Every one of these boys is a soloist in his own right ... as you could probably tell from that number/set.

It is said that the ideal wife for a musician would be a deaf-and-dumb blonde nymphomaniac who keeps a pub near a golf-course ...

The poet Congreve maintained that music hath charms to soothe the savage breast, and one violinist once thought he would put this saying to the test, so he packed his fiddle and took a boat to the Zambesi. There he paddled upstream for three hundred miles, then stepped ashore in the thickest, densest part of the forest he could find. And there he began to play. And pretty soon, there fell a hush in that part of the jungle, as all the animals stopped to listen. They crept forwards, and soon there, in a small clearing, the musician was surrounded by hundreds of animals and birds of all kinds, fascinated by the strains of that old fiddle. But then suddenly the spell was broken by a beaten-up, scarred old crocodile, who waddled up to the violinist and – CHOMP! – swallowed him up in one bite. 'What did you do that for?' said a lion. 'We were all enjoying that!' And the crocodile said, (*putting one hand to your ear*) 'Eh ... ?'

Some wonderful news, folks. This week our band leader's wife presented him with a bouncing baby boy! So will the proud father take a bow, please? (*All the rest of the band should rise and bow with the leader, 'unseen' by him*)

27

New Year Party

Enjoying yourselves . . . ? I'm certainly enjoying myself
. . . Well, there's no-one else here to enjoy. Still, the night is
young . . . Remember last year's party? Hands up all those
who were here last year . . . ? Wasn't it hell . . . ? No, I'm
only kidding – it was great. As the New Year came in, I
went out, like a light. Mind you, I never usually drink on
New Year's Eve – that's amateur night.

Someone once said [1] that there are two reasons for drinking: one is when you are thirsty – to cure it; the other, when
you are not thirsty, to prevent it. My sentiments, precisely,
and don't worry if you find yourself a little the worse for
wear – just don't worry about that. Do you know what I
take for a hangover? Do you know what I take for a hangover? Ten pints of strong ale and six double Scotches . . .
then I top it up with a bottle of Cyprus sherry . . . sweet
Cyprus sherry . . .

By the way, before I go any further, I have a message
for the couple who came . . . er . . . (*looking at piece of
paper*) . . . from (*local*) in a horse and buggy . . . over there?
The message is from the horse . . . he says (*reading*) can he
have his oats now – you can have yours later . . . ?

Of course, Scotland's the place to be for Hogmanay. I
remember one New Year party I went to there which was
also a fancy dress party. One girl turned up wearing nothing
– nothing – except a pair of black gloves and a pair of black
boots. I said to her, 'So what have you come as?' She said,
'The five of spades . . .'

It's going to be a great year, I'm sure of it – an historic
year, too. This year sees the tenth anniversary of Brian
losing his hair [2] and Bessie losing her . . . cherrywood beads
. . . On March 1st this year Julian will be taking his biennial
bath, and on April 15th Maurice has his triennial haircut.
Old Moore in his Almanac says that in June Roger will be

buying a new mac, but I think that's very unlikely. August sees Miriam's twenty-ninth birthday . . . again . . . and on October 1st one of the wives here tonight will have a baby . . . (*look at watch*) should be starting about now, fellas . . . anyone missing? In November Gavin will achieve the ambition of a lifetime – sit down, Tina – a week's holiday bird-watching in the Rotherhithe Tunnel [3] . . . The end of the year sees another very important anniversary – on December 31st we'll all be here getting blotto again . . . !

But have you made your New Year resolutions? [4] I'm going to lead a more sober and industrious life for a start . . . no, it's true. I had an uncle once who died of wine, women and song . . . what happened was he was singing this dirty song under a married bird's window and her husband came out and clocked him with a bottle of Wincarnis. No, actually, I've promised myself never again to drink on an empty stomach – in future I'll always have a couple of beers first. Hymie has resolved to take that trip to Israel – he wants to go to the Wailing Wall and join all the United supporters. Dorothy tells me she has decided to stop smoking in bed. I said, 'I didn't know you smoked cigarettes?' And Ken said, 'She doesn't – it's haddock . . .' Wally is going to strain every nerve to win this year's Russell Harty Charm Bracelet for Trying Not To Top Other People's Jokes. Margo's going to take ugly pills for the whole year to give the other girls a chance, and Frank is coming off the ugly pills . . . at least I hope so, Frank – enough is enough . . .

Well, I hope you all enjoy the party, and if you don't – well, you can just (*mime the rude word of your choice*) off! Happy New Year!

Suggested Headings

Enjoying yourselves? No-one else here to enjoy.
Hands up.
As New Year came in I went out. Amateur night.
Two reasons for drinking. When you are thirsty, to cure it.
When you are not thirsty, to prevent it.

For hangover: 10 pints, six Scotches and a bottle of (sweet) Cyprus Sherry.

Message to couple from (*local*) in horse and buggy. Oats now, yours later.

Scotland for Hogmanay.

Girl in nothing but black gloves and boots – five of spades.

Historic year: 10th anniversary of Brian losing his hair and Bessie losing her . . . cherrywood beads.

March 1st. Julian takes biennial bath.

April 15th. Maurice triennial haircut.

Old Moore's Almanac. In June Roger buying a new mac (unlikely).

August. Miriam's 29th birthday.

October 1st. One of wives present will have a baby.

November: Gavin will achieve ambition of lifetime (Tina). Week's bird-watching in (*local*).

December 31st. All here again getting blotto.

Resolutions. Me – more sober and industrious. Uncle who dies of wine, women and song. Never again drink on an empty stomach/couple of beers first.

Hymie to Israel – Wailing Wall – to join United supporters.

Dorothy no more smoking in bed. Ken – Haddock.

Wally. Russell Harty Charm Bracelet for Trying Not To Top Other People's Jokes.

Margo. Ugly pills.

Frank. Coming off ugly pills.

Hope you enjoy the party.

Notes

1. For the pedant, it was Thomas Love Peacock (1785–1886) who said this.
2. This whole paragraph is intended to show the kind of gags you might invent about the guests at your party. I think six quick one-line cracks are probably enough.
3. Gavin must be well-known for his fanatical dedication to his hobby. You will then set this in an unlikely setting, e.g. hang gliding on the M4 or skin diving in the number one theatre, St. Thomas's Hospital, London S.E.1. . . .

163

4. The resolutions, like the anniversaries, will also be based upon the known foibles and interests of your guests. Again I think half a dozen references are enough – although you can always prepare more and be ready to cut to the end if and when you feel interest flagging.

Keep this speech short and pithy. Remember your guests, and very likely yourself, will be largely inebriated by the time you come to deliver your oration so don't expect an attentive or patient audience. For this reason I would advise against your attempting to tell jokes as such – no-one will have the inclination to concentrate on stories. Just keep to one-line quickies and remarks about those present. You can, I think, be pretty outrageous on this occasion and not worry too much about offending – you can always say you were drunk. Which will probably be true. On the other hand, if you are really drunk you are in no condition to give a speech, so make up your mind to stay reasonably sober until *after* you have delivered your oration.

28

Odds & Ends: Old Time Music Hall

Introductions to the show

(*Entering to 'A Fine Old English Gentleman*)' My lords, ladies and gentlemen – good evening! . . . I know you're there, I can hear you breathing . . . My lords, ladies and gentlemen – GOOD EVENING! . . . and may I bid you a forthright and hearty welcome to this Cellar of Salubrity, this Hall of Remembrance . . . wherein the management proudly presents a lively and varied programme for you this evening, every item of which can be positively certified to be fit for family viewing, and guaranteed not to bring so much as the vestige of a blush to the most maidenly cheek. In other words, if you're a virgin, you'll love it. What the rest of you are going to make of it I'm not so sure. I shall be playing both ends against the middle as usual . . .

Yes, we have a mixed bag for you this evening . . . (*looking at fob watch*) she should be here about half-past nine . . . but first of all I must introduce myself. I have the pleasure and privilege of taking the chair and introducing the artistes throughout the entire performance. My name is (*name*) . . . thank you for that burst of indifference. I've just finished a Music Hall in Scunthorpe (*or local*) and now I've come to finish it off here. The doors are locked – you can't get out . . .

Tonight we take you back to the good old days – remember the good old days, dear? . . . when you could get drunk for a penny and dead drunk for twopence. And for a ha'penny – a ha'penny, ladies and gentlemen – you could get enough bile beans to keep you on the run for a month [1] . . .

Now, I'd just like to say, whatever you may think of the show – you've paid your money so you might as well make the best of it! Sauce . . . Yes, we're all set to experience the second best way of enjoying an evening . . . and if you have to ask what is the best – it's too late. Now then . . . oh, yes, first of all I must introduce our orchestra . . . here, obliging on the Steinway is our own one-man pianist – actually we should have had a three-piece but they only knew two pieces – so here he is playing not only on the black and not only on the white notes but also on the cracks in between . . . as you could probably tell from the overture. Ladies and gentlemen, Maestro (*name*)! Are you well, Maestro? Are you sober? That makes a change . . . Never mind – we're all on your side . . . so far . . .

Now, we come to our first chorus song, traditionally led by your chairman . . . Do you all have your song sheets? . . . and can you all read? If my old mother could see me now – she'd be so ashamed . . . she thinks I'm in prison . . . The song sheets have been printed in English for your convenience, and I would like you to turn your collective attention to number one inscribed thereon, a charming little aria I wrote myself while waiting for a laugh on Monday and entitled, 'She Was Only a Newsagent's Daughter, But She Liked Her Daily Mail.' Start pedalling, vicar.

(*Chairman leads the audience in a popular chorus*)

Ladies and gentlemen, with my hand on my heart and with all the sincerity at my disposal may I say that was absolutely . . . *frightful!* . . . You'll have to improve on that before I allow any artistes to step before you. Perhaps you'd all like to clear your throats before we attempt that once again . . . oh, how disgusting. I don't have to do this for a living, you know. I've got two chinchillas on heat . . . Let's try a little tune-up, then, Maestro, can we have a suitable tune-up note? (*pianist plays an A*) Lovely touch, that boy . . . we've got one at home just like that . . . Come on now: Lalalalaaaaa . . . strewth – from here it looked like a dentist's nightmare . . . and again . . . lalalalaaaa . . . I've just seen more bridgework than Brunel . . . and again . . . lalalalaaaa . . . Do you ever wish you'd never started something? Come on, sing up or I'll come round with a big whip and – oh, no – you might enjoy that . . . well, just do your best. Thank you, Maestro.

(Chairman leads the audience in a repeat of the same chorus)

Well done – give yourselves a round of applause ... and when we come to subsequent choruses please remember to keep your vowels open – that's very important ... And *that*! *(banging table with gavel)* ... I'm ruining my knocker ... brings us to the first item in the programme proper, so let us welcome ...

Notes

I offer no suggested headings for this speech, since it should be delivered without notes. The subject of the role of the Chairman in an Old Time Music Hall is an exceedingly complex and interesting one, and I have dealt with it fully in my book *It Gives Me Great Pleasure* (Samuel French 1972). This Chairman's handbook also lists some six hundred one-liners and patter entries, similar to the following:

Latecomers
I see the Tooting (*or local*) express is late again.
Did your horse throw a shoe?
Tillings are so unreliable, aren't they?
We've got more late entries than an Irish orchestra.
You're early for tomorrow night's show.

Intervals
(Before)
The Maestro and I will retire behind the arras, where we shall talk about you.
I'll have a much needed pint and the Maestro will have a pi ... anissimo.
(After)
Did you enjoy the interval? ... best part of the evening, I always think.
We were to have started the second half with the Dance of the Three Virgins ... but unfortunately they've broken their contract.

Will the owner of Hackney Carriage licence number X237WER947HS829 . . .QPROONBGPDQ1212999VHF please move it immediately as the number plate is blocking the carriageway.

Miss Helen Hunt, our box office manageress, has found a wallet containing a sum of money and various personal items – I think she said there was a packet of balloons among them . . . so if you have lost your wallet, you can go to Helen Hunt for it.

End of Show

I'd like to thank you from the bottom of my cheque book.
You've been a wonderful audience – and I'm hard to please
Thanks for having me, and for those who haven't, please be patient.
I'd like to thank his worship the Mayor of (*local*) without whose help this show would almost certainly have got on.
Goodnight – sweet dreams. I like dreaming, don't you?
You meet a nicer class of person that way.
I've got good news for you – it's pouring down outside . . .
No, I'm only kidding – it's snowing.
It isn't generally known but all the proceeds from tonight's performance, including the bar takings, will tomorrow morning be going straight to – Messrs. Barclays Bank.

Introductions for men

He has entertained at Buckingham Palace, I believe – or he mumbled something to me about being detained for Her Majesty's pleasure.
Here now from all the leading Music and Billiard Halls in the vicinity.
The last time he was here we saw him as a very sophisticated performer, very sophisticated – but he's been taking the tablets so he's all right now.
Here now in the first rosy flush of asphyxia.
Performing almost entirely from memory.

Exits for men

He has just returned from a tour of Arabian harems,

although the tour was curtailed – he just wasn't cut out for it.

You must admit he is very loyal to his material.

He has just done six weeks at the Savoy Hotel – looking for the gents.

He also does bird impressions – he eats worms.

Some artistes may be one in a thousand – he was won in a raffle.

He has a vast repertoire, and having shared a dressing room with him I'm in a position to know just how vast that is.

Introductions for women

The art of Bel Canto will now be demonstrated in all its glory by . . .

Here now, a feast for the eye and the ear . . .

That wearer of the face serene and bearer of the form divine.

This artiste is much sought after and I believe much yearned after.

Miss N will be arrayed in a somewhat revealing costume but, gentlemen, please try to keep yourselves in hand.

'*Who Were You With Last Night?*' cries our next artiste accusatorially in number X, on your race-ca . . . song-sheets.

So you married men, if you fancy a flighty philandering flutter, beware the eagle eye of Miss N.

'*I'll Make A Man Of You*,' declares our next artiste, a song made famous by the surgical registrar of St. Thomas's Hospital . . . There will be no blood-letting tonight – at least I hope not – but, gentlemen, you will be now well and truly operated upon by Miss N.

Exits for women

She told me she's just got engaged to an Irishman. I said, 'Oh, really?' She said, 'No – O'Reilly . . .'

She used to be married to a trapeze artist but she caught him in the act.

(*After a frank display of feminine charms*) I've seen nothing like it since I was weaned *or* I suddenly fancy a milk stout – I don't know why *or* I wish it was the interval *or* I really had to keep a grip on myself.

(*After 'train' number*) Miss N will always have a permanent way in our hearts *or* now there's a girl worth taking a sleeper from Waterloo to New Cross for (*or local stations close together*).
I used to have a crush on her but she pushed me off.
I was nearly carried away then and that's not a pretty sight.
Every time I see Miss N I reach for my Iron Jelloids.

General introductions
This artiste needs no encomium from me.
... to be sung affectingly and effectively by ...
... now to be rendered to the utmost advantage by ...
Saved in the nick of time from the taxidermist.
To give us a taste of his/her quality.
I'm sure you'll find this item as awe-ful as I do.
Here now in blush-pink and 3/4 time.
Here now dressed in some of the less well-known items from the (*name of theatre or society*) wardrobe.
Snatched from the jaws of the Albert Hall.
That fine artiste, whose talent is commensurate with his/her charm and good looks, none other than (*look at list*) Charlie Farnsbarns???
One of the finest artistes in the country. Lousy in town but great in the country.
(*For speciality act*) A feat unparalleled since the discovery of chloroform.
Let us now meet and greet ...
In our shows beforehand this artiste has so often been tried, tested and – found wanting.
At this point in the programme we usually have the interval, only tonight it is called Mr N ...
I won't say too much about the next act – this is a clean show.

Here's an act which is rapidly becoming an institution – and some say that's where he/she belongs.

General exits

Very touching . . . especially towards the end of the week.

That artiste appeared by courtesy of money.

Ah, well that's got that over.

Wasn't he/she wonderful? I knew him/her when he/she was alive.

What could possibly follow that turn other than the end of the world? So let us now enjoy our internationally re-nowned interval. I'm sure we'd all like to wish him/her the best of good fortune with his/her forthcoming tour of the Goodwin Sands (*or local*).

I'm sure you'd like to know that that act was passed by the Lord Chamberlain and the number thirteen bus.

I didn't book him.

That act was rather like soup de jour – you never know what to expect.

I'm sure we would all agree that that artiste has the makings of a great failure.

He/she used to be a tap dancer, but he/she kept falling in the sink.

He's/she's wonderful for his/her age . . . only twenty-three (*after 'old age' number*).

That was N making his/her debacl – debut, I mean.

As ever performing with style, wit and insouciance . . . Do you know what insouciance means? So much for compul-sory education . . .

Duet gags

They used to work as the Brothers Zola – Emile and Gorgon.

Their names are N and N – I don't know which is which but I'm told that they do.

Sketch gags

Try not to cry in your beer – it's watered already.

We present now our trau-dramatic sketch.

171

Ladies take hold of your hankies and gentlemen take hold of your ladies.
(*After*) Now let that be a terrible warning to you.

Heckle-stoppers
Why don't you go home? – your cage'll be cleaned out by now.
It's people like you that turn acts into agents.
Oh shut up . . . That's what they call repartee . . .
I've never believed in Darwin's theory but now I'm not so sure.
Why weren't you at rehearsals?
Order in the marijuana section, please.
Would you mind having your nervous breakdown somewhere else?
He's as sharp as a tack . . . Anyone got a hammer?
He's a case . . . Mind you don't get nailed up.

The above is a selection of some of the less hackneyed Music Hall one-liners; it is always best to think up your own, especially should you endeavour to relate an introduction to the content of the act, the costume, the lyrics, etc.

172

29

Odds & Ends: Horror Night

In October 1973 I was asked to assume the role, complete with costume and greenish make-up, of Dracula in order to compere a 'Horror' night in the Sculptor Room at Woburn Abbey. This event was to be in aid of REHAB. I questioned the organizer closely on the items in the evening's programme, and devised the following speech:

(As the participants enter, ghostly music is heard in the dimly-lit room; on a dais at one end of the long high and narrow chamber, with its pillars and statues, lies a coffin, illuminated by a spotlight. When all are seated, the lights suddenly go out, except for the spotlight, the music gives way to screams and groans, and the lid of the coffin is suddenly and violently thrown back. In the ensuing tense silence, the figure within sits up, gazes round, smiles in an eerie, sinister fashion, and steps out, advancing slowly to the regrettably mundane microphone. Then Count Dracula – for it is he – speaks)

Aaah ... I've been expecting you ... I needed that sleep – I've been so occupied lately ... I have the honour to welcome you here tonight to this historic house. I love the decor [1] ... just think of all the generations who have died here ... it gives me quite a thrill ...

I am your host, my name is Count Dracula and I sincerely hope that you all have a most hideous evening as we present for you a night of Magic and Mystery. We started off with the Magic and Mystery of the Blue Bonnets Pipe Band [2] – the magic is how they play those things and the mystery is why anyone should want to listen to such barbaric instruments ... it's enough to wake the dead ...

For the next hour or so, please make yourselves well and truly at home – some of you won't be going back. At ten o'clock we die – dine ... sorry, just a slip of the fang ...

and until then a bar will cater for those in need of a little stimulant in this room to the rear on the right. In the chamber on the opposite side is a tombola stall with dozens of magnificent prizes. The first prize is a week's holiday for two at my castle in Transylvania . . . the second prize is two weeks holiday at my castle in Transylvania . . .

Then there is a photographer present with an instant camera should you wish to have your likeness recorded with myself – not that I am visible, of course, on photographic reproductions – and we also have members of the Magic Circle who will mingle amongst you performing magic under your noses. Ladies, keep a tight grip on your handbags and gentlemen, keep a tight grip on your ladies . . .

In the temple at the rear we are privileged to have with us tonight two celebrated lady mediums. They are quite genuine – and I should know – and are Madame Mareeb Amarna and Madame Mereeta. These ladies, both of whom are Egyptian priestesses – are available for brief consultations, so should you wish to contact the other side, please give your name to the temple guard and you will be called over . . .

Finally, a full list of events is included in our souvenir lucky programmes which are available from our fetchingly-clad Bunny Girls. I love those costumes – the way they reveal the girl's necks – it makes them so appetizing. The programmes are all numbered and the winner – gets out alive. Just my little joke . . . in fact the winner will receive a magnificent Colour Television set. They are really marvellous sets, I have one myself. The colour is so lifelike – especially blood.

Well, now, as I said, we dine at ten – I love having people for dinner. So until then enjoy yourselves . . . while you can.

(*At ten o'clock, Dracula announces:*) Ladies and gentlemen, a sumptuous repast is now being served – a banquet to tickle the palate of the most fastidious gourmet . . . except of course there is no garlic . . . please be seated.

(*At the end of the evening:*) It is time for us to part. Your carriages are waiting and as for me – I must fly . . . We thank you for coming, and when you are lying in your beds tonight, and you hear strange noises, you hear strange bumps and tappings at your window, you sense a ghostly presence, you see strange apparitions – remember, there *are* such things [3] . . . (*disappearing*) . . . goodnight . . .

Notes

1. The organizers had decorated the room with skeletons, bats, etc.
2. The participants had come from London by coach, and were met by the Blue Bonnets (City of London) Pipe Band.
3. I actually saw Bela Lugosi play Dracula on stage, and he made a curtain speech on the lines of my last paragraph. As he spoke, mist began to appear around his feet and he seemed to disappear in a swirl of ectoplasm.

The point of my quoting the opening speech is to show how it fulfilled three objectives : (a) to impart the necessary information (the photographer, the mediums, the tombola, the magicians, etc., also that the meal would be at a certain time); (b) to establish and maintain the character of Dracula; (c) to be funny. I am happy to tell you that this speech – and I haven't altered one syllable – was extremely well received and got the evening off to an appropriate and stylish start.

30

Odds & Ends: King Arthur's Court

In June 1975 I was engaged by a firm of conference organizers to appear as 'Lord Chamberlain' in a Night at the Court of King Arthur which they were arranging for five hundred American salesmen and their wives at the Hilton Hotel. The actual start of the evening was a complicated affair involving the top salesman pulling the Sword from the Stone (it got stuck and was only released after several very strained minutes during which your author had to ad-lib . . .) and being crowned King by Merlin – the well-known magician, John Wade, essayed this role. It was then necessary for me to address the assemblage to inform them what the evening had in store, and of course I had to stand around and make myself generally available for any required announcements. As with the previous 'Dracula' speech I had to get over some hard information but in a humorous manner consistent with the theme of the evening. Eventually I concocted the following:

(*Fanfare*)
In order to ensure a night of carousel, wassail and good cheer, I command thee upon a count of three to turn to thy neighbour on thy right and then to thy neighbour on thy left and say, 'Hail, neighbour!' or 'How art thou?' or 'Neeeagh' . . . after three . . . (*bangs staff*) Three!

My lords and ladies, in a right royal court there are certain niceties of behaviour and points of etiquette to be observed which I shall now acquaint you with (*unrolls parchment*):
Item – Do not quit ye Great Hall with reverencing to Their Majesties. Ye retiring-rooms are to be found through the ante-chamber whence ye entered. Ye ladies' room is on ye right and their lordships are accommodate on ye left.

Shouldst thou confuse the rooms it may be embarrassing but think of the friends thou wilt make.

Item – All ye Jester's witticisims must be laughed at on pain of the pillory – missiles will be provided. And ye Jester's witticisms are humorous in truth – Master Joe Miller hath writ them all down.

Item – Do not use thy platter to batter thy neighbour's skull.

Item – Throw thy meat bones over thy right shoulders only.

Item – Your lordships must restrain from pawing ye serving wenches, at least until after ye banquet.

Item – Your lordships must further restrain from pawing thy neighbour's wife, unless he be too drunk to care. Or too sober to care.

Item – Do not wipe thy greasy fingers on thy neighbour's doublet – or on his singlet, for that matter.

Item – On no account may your lordships unsheathe thy weapons at the table.

During the sumptuous repast which is e'en now on its way to you, we have divers goodly entertainments prepared for thee, namely:

Ye Jester, Will Japes, will somersault across forty-two barrels of mead . . . a sort of medieval Knievel.

Ye court wizard, yclept Merlin, and his apprentice Tricky Dicky will come among thee demonstrating their digital dexterity, so watch thyselves, ladies . . . your lordships might have a care also . . .

A group of minstrels, Morris Dancer and the Maypoles will regale thee with songs from the Camelot Top Ten.

The mighty Reuben, our pocket Goliath, will perform feats of strength unparalleled since Samson brought ye house down.

A damsel of sweet voice and even sweeter parts will present one of the lays of old England.

John Allthumbs, the jongleur, will juggle his balls most dexterously – a truly wondrous sight.

177

And finally there will be dancing to the dulcet strains of (*name*) and his Celtic Stompers.

Thou hast already seen our fire-eater, Tongueless Thomas, who is now in ye kitchen helping to keep ye joint warm.

Which brings me back to the Lucullan feast of which thou art about to partake. We were to have started with soup of ye tomato, but we discovered that ye master cook is a vampire . . . however, all ye victuals are of ye very finest quality. I have been to ye kitchens myself, my lords and ladies, and ten thousand flies cannot be wrong.

So now, let revelry be unconfined and let ye banquet commence! (*Fanfare*)

Notes

I persuaded the organizers to let me engage a small brass-player (I am extremely tall) who, dressed in a tabard, followed me everywhere and blew fanfares on a posthorn when ever I wanted attention. We were able to work out some comedy business – primitive but effective – so he provided some laughs as well as providing a decorative and utilitarian function.

The difficulty with these large functions is always to capture attention, which is why most of the entertainment was peripatetic, i.e. the minstrels and magicians wandered round the tables. The other 'turns' were spectacular – fire-eating, the strong man (who used volunteers from the audience) and a marvellous sword-fight between two 'knights'.

I must confess that not all my speech was used – the organizers thought some of it too racy for middle-class Americans and their wives, and some of it seemed irrelevant when I actually came to deliver it. But I quote it here *in toto* to give an idea of how to approach this kind of speech.

31

Presentation: Proposal

Well, ladies and gentlemen, I suppose you're wondering why I've called you all here ... It is of course to do honour to our highly esteemed colleague Jasper Porklebay and to present him with the 19— Bob Monkhouse Golden Dimple for Quick Thinking [1] ...

Jasper was born at a very early age, and when his mother presented his father with that precious little pink bundle, it was seen straight away that Jasper was something special – he was already wearing an eye-shade and practising a riffle shuffle [2] ... At the time his parents were in the Iron and Steel industry – mother ironed and father stole ... so there was plenty of money and the young Master Porklebay was sent to Eton ... Approved Sch – er, a school in Berkshire of which everyone approved. On one celebated occasion when asked by the teacher where Leeds was, our Jasper replied 'top of the First Division, sir!' [3] When asked what was the order of the Bath, answered, 'Well, first it's me Mum, then me Dad, then me sister and then me.' Occasionally it must be admitted, he skipped school entirely, but when taxed about this replied in his customary forthright and unequivocal manner that he had been sick. 'Sick of what?' asked the head. 'Sick of school ...' came the reply.

On leaving school he spent two years as a National Serviceman in the Scunthorpe Fusiliers, leaving with a very good record – Maria Callas singing highlights from 'Carmen.' [4] After which he joined us here at Sweatshops Ltd since when we've been trying to get rid – no! – we've been very appreciative of his contributions to the profitability and smooth running of the firm. Why only last week the Chairman saw him crossing the road outside and said to me, 'Who *is* that ... ?' [5]

We shall miss you – won't we, Gina? [6] – not only in the office but also at our social activities and on the sports field. I well remember the occasion when you were batting in the Sweatshops First Eleven and I was umpire in that match against Hammer & Sickle. I gave you out and you took it on the chin like the sportsman you are. You just turned to me and said, 'What for?' [7] I said, 'For the rest of the afternoon . . .' Then there was the time he was refereeing a football match when our team was playing an eleven from Datchet (*or local*). He blew up for a free kick and when the opposing captain said, 'Who for?' He said 'Us . . .' But he's also a pretty fair golfer . . . if you keep your eye on him.

I think even Jasper would admit that his efforts with the Dramatic Society were not too successful. The last show he was in we charged 25p to get in and 50p to get out . . . made a fortune . . . Mind you, Jasper's been in films, you know. Did you see (*latest box office sensation*)? So did I – jolly good, wasn't it . . . ?

That was a bit of a facer when you had that accident last year Jasper . . . strained groin, wasn't it? Never sure what that is, anyway . . . the office just wasn't the same when you came back . . . Sorry, I'll read that again. 'The office just wasn't the same.' When you came back . . . you told me you'd asked the doctor for something to make you sweat, and he'd signed you off . . . But Jasper is a self-made man (which is a good trick if you've got the agility) . . . and I know he will continue to rule in our hearts and affections. He has always been generous – remember the time he bought a round in the club? The secretary has carved the date on the bar . . . and of course he's very broad-minded. In fact he tells me he thinks of little else . . .

But he's also a careful man – even looks both ways before crossing his legs – and he tells me that since being with us he has saved £5,000! Mind you, last week his great aunt died and left him £4,972 . . . But we're sure, Jasper, that you'll remain the same dear, unspoiled, unselfish, compassionate – am I overdoing it, d'you think? [8] – chap you've always been . . . and so now I have the pleasure, on behalf of all of us, to wish you the best of luck and to present you with this (*whatever*) as a token of our affection and regard.

Suggested Headings

Wondering why/to do honour to JP and present him with 19— Bob Monkhouse Golden Dimple for Quick Thinking.

Born at an early age/straight away something special – eye-shade and practising riffle-shuffle.

Parents in Iron and Steel Trade.

Eton – Approved Sch –.

Where's Leeds? Top of 1st Division.

Order of the Bath? Mum, Dad, sister, then me.

Occasionally missed school/sick/ of what? Of school!

Nat Service in Scunthorpe Fusiliers. Good record – Callas in 'Carmen'.

Then joined us since when we've been trying to get rid – no, appreciative.

Last week. Chairman: Who *is* that?

Miss you, won't we, Gina?

Cricket: you batting/me umpire. Out. What for? Rest of the afternoon.

Refereeing football match. Blew for free kick. Who for? Us.

Fair golfer. If you keep your eye on him.

Not too successful with ADS. 25p to get in and 50p to get out.

Been in films. See (*latest sensation*)? So did I.

Accident last year – strained groin.

Office wasn't the same when you came back. Read again.

Something to sweat. Doctor signed you off.

Setlf-made man. Generous/bought round/date carved on bar.

Broad-minded.

Careful. Looks both ways before crossing his legs.

Saved £5,000. Left £4,972 by great-aunt.

Dear, unspoiled, unselfish, compassionate. Overdoing it?

Pleasure to wish you best of luck.

Notes

1. This joke award should reflect some trifling defect in the recipient's character, i.e. if he is known to be clumsy or

181

inelegant, it could be the Margot Fonteyn China Bull for Grace and Poise.

2. This would refer to a predilection for poker. It is not difficult to invent similar nonsensical instances for whatever hobbies or interests your recipient is known for.

3. This reference to football should be altered to incorporate the recipient's known passion. An alternative might be, 'When asked who signed the Magna Carta, he replied, "It wasn't me, sir!"'

4. National Service was abolished in 1960 and so does not apply to men born after 1942.

5. 'Who *is* that?' should be said in tones of utter distaste.

6. Gina will be the office Circe.

7. 'What for?' should be said in outraged indignation, laced with naked aggression. This will then contrast nicely with the calm, gentle build-up.

8. This should be said to some one close to you but *not* to the recipient.

The object of a speech like this one is to include as many of the recipient's foibles as possible, without being too hurtful. If the presentation is being made to a lady you must be that much more careful; a gentler and more straightforward approach is recommended. When my wife left the BBC after twelve years in the Drama Department (in order to have a baby) her boss made a most charming speech at her farewell party, slightly fulsome as is expected on these occasions, and referring to her unfortunate tendency to arrive late in the mornings. This tiny pinprick was extremely well received and helped to allay the inevitable cloying nature of speeches at this kind of function.

The following might be of possible use:

Before coming to us, Jasper used to be a real live wire salesman – he sold live wires.

I gave him a little test when he first applied for a job here. I said,' What's twelve times twelve?' He said, 'One hundred and forty-four.' I said, 'That's good.' He said, 'Good – it's perfect!'

One morning he arrived very late, so I said to him, 'You should have been here at nine o'clock.' He said, 'Why – what happened?'

Then another time he was late so I said, 'What is it this time?' He said, 'My father has been burnt.' I said, 'Oh, I'm sorry to hear that. Is it serious?' He said, 'Well, they don't muck about at the crematorium . . .'

32

Presentation: Reply

Thank you for those kind remarks. I can only say . . . it's all true, every word of it . . . But you know when I first came here, from the great Metrollops of Stow-in-the-Hold (*or local*) I was very anxious. In fact I was so frightened, on my first morning I very nearly shatt . . . ered my self confidence beyond repair . . . But you were all so very kind and understanding . . . even Nobby gave me a friendly sniff [1] . . .

Well, you see I've always been very shy and modest . . . Yes, I know, I've got a lot to be modest about . . . But I'm an only child . . . when I was born my parents took one look at me and decided they couldn't possibly improve on Nature . . . But you were all so nice and helpful. Even Mr. Flack was sympathetic after I'd been late three mornings in a row. I told him the bus kept running late so he said, 'Well, if it's late again tomorrow catch an earlier one . . .'

Mr Flak was the reason I joined this firm actually. I'd rather wanted to be a sex maniac but the competition was too stiff. And then I saw Mr Flak and I thought to myself, 'Gosh, I'd like to be like him – smart and sophisticated and respected and rich . . . if that's what being in (*whatever*) does for a man, show me where to sign.' But he can be tough, can't he? I remember once he said to me, 'Answer the phone.' I said, 'But Slimy,' I said [2] . . . 'it's not ringing.' He said, 'Well, why leave everything till the last minute . . . ?' One thing that helped me here was experience in book-keeping . . . why, I've had some library books for over five years . . . but I had a bad start, I must admit. When I was being interviewed I naturally asked the salary and was told it was £30 a week with another £10 a week in six months. So I said, 'Right – I'll come back in six months . . .' Old Charlie did laugh at that one [3] . . .

My first morning could have been my last, though. The phone rang. I answered it and Mr Flak said, 'What is it?' I said, 'I think you're wanted, sir.' He said, 'What do you mean – you think?' I said, 'Well, this chap said : is the old fool there . . . ?' But he took it very well, considering . . . and the convalescent home was very nice . . .

Everyone's been so kind to me . . . on the whole. I'd like to thank Bessie for making me a cup of tea every morning . . . and I'd like to thank Colin for drinking it. I'd like to thank Glenda for introducing me to good music [4] . . . and to Rick for all the advice without which I should probably still be – at least two grades higher.[5] I'd like to thank the Managing Director for the use of the hall, and all of you for being here today. I was given a presentation once before, actually – a season ticket to (*local*) crematorium.

But it really is marvellous of you all to have contributed your hard-earned pounds . . . silver . . . coppers for this marvellous (*whatever*), and all I can say is – why didn't you tell me, I'd have got you trade . . . No, it's great of you all and I'm very touched. Thanks very much.

Suggested Headings

It's true.

Metrollops. Very nervous/shattered.

Nobby. Sniff.

Shy and modest. Only child.

Flak sympathetic after late three mornings. Bus late.

Sex maniac.

Flak smart/sophisticated/respected/rich.

Answer the phone. Not ringing (Slimy).

Experience in book-keeping.

Interview : £20 + £10 in six months. Charlie laughed.

1st morning : Phone – is the old fool there?

Everyone so kind, on the whole

Bessie made tea. Colin drinking it.

Glenda. Good music.

Rick for advice. Two grades higher.

Thank MD for use of the hall.

Presentation once before. Season ticket to (*local*) crematorium.

Marvellous of you all to have contributed.
Very touched.

Notes
1. Nobby's sniff will have been a source of amusement/
   irritation for years. Other foibles can be someone's tuneless whistle, tapping, winking, nudging, etc.
2. Slimy will be Mr Flak's nickname, Mr Flak himself
   being the manager.
3. Charlie will be someone extremely senior, like the
   Managing Director or the Chairman.
4. Glenda will be notorious for her addiction to pop music.
5. Rick will be the office know-all.

You will need to give your own version of your career
with the firm, listing your difficulties, embarrassments and
promotions. Canteen food, changes in the Board, divi-
dends, foreign trade – all can be utilized. I'd keep off
politics and union matters unless you are senior enough to
be sure of your ground – you don't want your presentation
to lead to a shut-down of the firm.

The following might be of use:
I well remember my first annual leave: On the Friday
afternoon just as I was leaving Mr Crabby said to me,
'Enjoy yourself, Porklebay, because when you come back
I shall have something very serious to say to you . . .' You
can imagine how much I enjoyed *that* holiday. Do you
know what he wanted to say that was so serious? Instead
of watering his plants twice a week I had to do it three
times a week . . .'
Mr Crabby was very tough, though. When I first came
here he summoned me into his office and said, 'Now, boy,
cleanliness is essential in this business. Have you wiped
your feet on the mat?' I said, 'Yes, sir.' He said. 'And the
other essential thing in this business is truthfulness – there
is no mat . . .' In fact I left my last job after something the
boss said. He wasn't abusive – he just said, 'You're sacked'.

33

Promotion: Proposal

Your attention, ladies and gentlemen, please. Well, George, you've pulled it off . . . no, it's a promotion richly deserved . . . you've studied for it, worked for it, crawled – no! . . . richly deserved, as I said. You've really come on wonderfully since you first came to us, a callow spotty adolescent dressed in a purple zoot suit with black velvet cuffs and crepe wedgies.[1] You used to wear a pork pie hat, if I remember, but the gravy kept running down your ears . . . Nowadays, of course, you always dress so well, and I heard one of the girls say the other day you always dress so quickly as well.

But, ladies and gentlemen, this polished, poised – one might say finished – young man swaying before us today was so green when he first entered this firm.[2] I remember shortly after he started with us he came in very excited one day with a book he'd just bought off a second-hand stall. It was called, 'How to Hug', which in those far-off pre-permissive days was a pretty fruity title. 'Let's have a look,' I said to him. Well, I didn't want him to read anything that might worry or upset him . . . and I read 'How to Hug, volume vi, Collin's Graphic English Dictionary . . .'

We did have some trouble with his punctuality in those days, I remember. Mind you, he was just the same at school; in fact I was told that when his headmaster asked him in front of the whole school why he was always rushing in to assembly after the bell, he replied, 'Because you always stop ringing it before I get there.' A perfectly logical answer, but then George is nothing if not logical. I well remember having to ask him his age for some form or other, and asking him what he would be on his next birthday. 'Twenty,' he replied and I said, 'So you were nineteen on your last birthday.' 'No,' he said, 'I was eighteen on my last birthday' . . . Do you remember this, George? . . .

No? I hope to goodness, I do . . . so I said, 'But if your next birthday is your twentieth your last must have been your nineteenth?' 'No,' he said, 'My nineteenth birthday is today' – you see what I mean about being logical . . . ?

But as I said, he soon became smart and attractive to the girls, so today we see him stylishly clothed in John Collier's best – I wonder what John Collier's wearing . . . and a roving bachelor of this parish . . . stud fee one-fifty plus VAT [3] . . .

Your career, George, has been marked by steady progress in the firm's esteem and in the golden opinions both of your juniors and your peers, and of course last year you won the Pete Murray Snigger Certificate for Services to Sycophancy – no! You swotted hard, passed your exams, kept your nose clean, watched and remained ready to learn. Your tact and diplomacy with customers and with your colleagues no less than your aptitude for (*whatever*) soon marked you out as a coming man, and who will ever forget the wit and grace of your famous remark to the wife of one of the directors at the annual dinner dance, when you said to her, 'Gosh, Mrs Gelt, you sweat less than any fat woman I've ever danced with . . .' Yes, it's little things like that will ensure your going far . . .like Scunthorpe [4] . . .

But in your new and exalted position we hope that you won't forget us serfs down here and that you will condescend to pay us a visit from time to time, if only to divvy up your last share of the tea kitty.

George, it's a well-deserved, well-merited promotion which reflects well not only upon you but upon our masters who make these decisions, and I am sure it will be but one of a long series of rungs in the ladder of success. Here's to you, and from all of us: good luck!

Suggested Headings

You've pulled it off.
Studied/worked/crawled.
Come on wonderfully since adolescence. Zoot suit.
Pork pie hat.

188

Now you dress so well and so quickly.

This polished, poised/finished young man was so green.

Book: How to Hug.

Trouble with punctuality. At school: 'Why always rushing in after bell?' 'Because you stop ringing it before I get here.'

Logical.

What age next birthday – 20/so last birthday 19/No – 18. I'm 19 today.

Smart and attractive in John Collier's best.

Roving bachelor. Stud fee £1.50+VAT.

Career marked by steady progress.

Pete Murray Snigger Certificate for Services to Sycophancy.

Swotted/passed exams/kept nose clean/watched and remained ready to learn.

Tact and diplomacy with customers and colleagues+aptitude marked you out.

Remark to director's wife: 'Gosh, Mrs Gelt, you sweat less than any fat woman I've ever danced with.'

That will ensure your going far/Scunthorpe.

In new and exalted position don't forget us/divvy up.

Well-deserved/well-merited/first of long series.

Notes

1. This costume was worn by Teddy boys in the early 1950's; the reference here should be to a similar outmoded fashion – Mods, Skinheads, Bovver Boys, Flower-Child, Peace Freaks, Arnolds, etc.

2. If alcohol is being served, you can add at this point: 'His colour's nothing to write home about today, by the look of him . . . has somebody been spiking his whisky with water . . . ? etc., etc.'

3. If 'George' is married this can be altered to include a reference to his wife, e.g. 'And married to a beautiful, charming, loving and very short-sighted wife – no!'

4. Scunthorpe here could be a far-away branch of the firm which is a notoriously unpopular posting.

Since this kind of speech is very often combined with a presentation, some aspects of the speech on page 179 can very likely be incorporated in this one. But don't be tempted to use all of my suggestions *and* your own bright ideas or you'll be on your feet for 40 minutes and kill the party stone dead. Remember – the more people have had to drink the less inclined they are to listen to speeches. See para 2 of *Timing* (page 12).

The following might be of use:

I once asked for a rise, and the manager – it was Mr Scrooge in those days – said, 'Why?' I said, 'Well, sir, my wife's having another baby.' He said, 'I'm not responsible for accidents which occur off the premises.'

I remember George asking for an afternoon off once, for his grandmother's funeral. I said, 'But you went to your grandmother's funeral only three months ago.' He said, 'I know, but grandfather got married again.'

We all hope that, despite George's elevation, he will still remain as enthusiastic as ever about the Football XI. As some of you may know, for some years George was always left outside, and for the past three seasons he has been a reliable drawback.

34

Promotion: Reply

Thank you, Sid, I hope I can do the same for you some day
... Well, boys and girls, it's really great of you all to come
here to celebrate my promotion – eat your heart out,
Peters.[1] I know I'll never forget this department . . . no
matter how hard I try . . . I'd like to say it's been wonderful
working with you all . . . I'd like to but I can't . . . No, I'm
only kidding . . . you hope. But how did I start here? I
came originally through my father – he's an exporter . . .
worked for the old Great Western . . . and he was keen for
me to get a good, steady, prestigious, well-paid job with
excellent prospects . . . so I worked for (*rival firm*) for two
years and then applied for a job here. They didn't want any
references, Mr Crabby just said, 'Well, if you can stick that
lot for two years you must be all right.'

So I was in – I had to find digs round here, my home was
a little place somewhere up around (*local*). I don't remember where exactly – I just blocked it out – and I walked
around banging on doors asking for accommodation.
Eventually the door of one little boarding house was
opened by this woman, quite fair she was – you know, forty
and fruity – no, not you, Martha . . . and she said, 'Yes,' I
said, 'Wait a minute, I haven't asked you yet . . .'

Anyway I was there for a few weeks until I moved into
a flat with . . . a friend . . . just a stone's throw from here.
You couldn't miss it – all the windows were broken. But I
was so unbelievably naive then . . . what do you mean, still
am . . . ? I used to think a brassiere was something to warm
your hands on.[2] Those of you interested in astrology, by
the way, will be interested to learn that I was born under
the sign 'No Smoking In Bed' – my parents were on holiday
at the time.

But everyone was so kind to me . . . and of course, as a
very junior junior my pay was appalling – in fact after three

months I was being picketed by Chinese coolies – but I especially remember how kind Mr Cringe was, giving me such helpful advice and encouragement as 'WHAT THE BLOODY HELL DO YOU THINK YOU'RE DOING!' [3] I mustn't forget Mrs Lush who showed me how to cook the – balance the books; Henry who taught me all those happy, lovable wheezes about sending the junior for a left-handed screwdriver or a tin of striped paint – how I laughed when I discovered I'd spent all day running round on a wild goose chase [4] . . . I must of course mention Darlene who so kindly initiated me into the mysterious, warm delights of . . . the stockroom . . . Yes, many's the happy hour Darlene and I have spent there, date-stamping the cat [5] and I am deeply grateful. When I told her I had a new position you can just imagine how thrilled she was . . .

My job will certainly mean more money – I've spent the first few week's extra on this suit. Do you like it? I got it backing a horse – backed it through Burton's window . . . But just getting paid more doesn't always mean you get more. I heard that one of the top salesmen was paying so much income tax that for his Christmas bonus he's getting a salary cut. Yes, it's tough at the top, but I am confident that with the support and training I have acquired here in this office, I'll be able to hold my own . . . if you'll pardon the expression.

As I've said, I'm really going to miss you, and as I climb the steep slope of success, if ever you're in need of a hand-out or a crust of bread or a bowl of warm gruel, don't hesitate to call – the Salvation Army any hour of the day or night.

Thank you again for your good wishes.

Suggested Headings

Hope I can do the same.
Great of you all to come. Eat your heart out Peters.
Never forget this dept. Like to say it's been wonderful. Only kidding. How did I start here?
Came here through father/exporter/old GWR.

Good, steady, prestigious, well-paid job with prospects (*rival firm*).

No references. Mr Crabby. If you can stick that lot.

Had to find digs. Can't remember home town. Blocked it out.

Landlady. 40 and fruity. 'Yes?'

Moved into flat with friend. Stone's throw.

Very naive then. Brassiere/something to warm your hands on.

Astrology. 'No Smoking in Bed' sign.

Everyone so kind. Appalling pay. Picketed by Chinese coolies.

Mr Cringe very kind. Advice and encouragement.

Mrs Lush. Cook/balance the books.

Henry. Left-handed screwdriver or tin of striped paint.

Darlene. Initiated me. Stockroom. Date-stamping the cat. New position. She was thrilled.

New job means more money. Like suit? Backing a horse.

Top salesman paying so much income tax.

Tough at the top but after here I'll be able to hold my own.

As I climb/if ever you're in need/Salvation Army.

Notes

1. Peters will be your rival for the job. This is a very cruel jest so be careful how you use it, if you use it.
2. Ideally this should be something which reflects the work in hand, i.e. in a men's-wear business you could say, 'I used to think that a jockstrap was a Scotsman's mouth.'
3. Mr Cringe will be someone well known in the department for his fiery temper. The words quoted should be one of Mr Cringe's regular expressions.
4. Your face should show that you *hated* being made a fool of.
5. 'Date-stamping the cat' should be altered to something apt for the nature of the business, i.e. a stationery firm could find you both 'counting the paper clips'.

As with the previous reply speech, you may well find

suitable material on page 186. Don't forget that a certain degree of proper sentiment should be shown; however exciting the new job seems to you, don't seem to eager to be shot of your old colleagues.

35

Retirement: Proposal

Well, Bill, you've done your bit . . . if you'll pardon the expression. Thirty years with one firm is a pretty good record, and for a man to put up with us all these years takes some doing. Actually, Bill nearly missed working for us altogether – he originally came here to clean the windows.[1] He was up on his ladder cleaning a certain window when he saw something he shouldn't have and he's been on the payroll ever since. I wonder if old C.B. still plays tiddleywinks [2] . . . ?

Of course, Bill, in your time you've seen a lot of changes – the canteen's had a coat of paint . . . Maurice has bought a new suit . . . the boys have got cheekier and the girls' dresses have got . . . well, Bill said to me only the other day as we watched Margie follolloping across the car-park, 'I wish I was forty years older . . .' I said, 'Don't you mean forty years younger?' he said, 'No forty years older – then I wouldn't give a damn . . .'

Anyway, we're going to miss you a very great deal, Bill. But there are compensations – your family will be seeing a great deal more of you – especially those grandchildren, eh? And perhaps now you will have the time to work for that marrow prize you've been after for so many years. Have you ever seen his marrow? It's enormous! [3] There are other compensations to being retired – free bus travel, cheap haircuts, free cinema seats in the afternoons, and best of all – you won't have to come here and shout at Bob to get a move on any more [4] . . .

It was the writer R. C. Sheriff who said, 'When a man retires and time is no longer of urgent importance, his colleagues generally present him with a clock.' Well, Bill, we're not going to give you a clock nor a watch nor even a sundial, but we do feel that 30 years of sterling and greatly valued service should be recognized, and so I have the pleasure and privilege, on behalf of the management and all your many friends in the firm, of presenting you with this (*whatever*). Use it for many years in good health, well done – and good luck!

Suggested Headings

Done your bit.
30 years a good record to put up with us.
Nearly missed working for us. Clean the windows.
CB plays tiddleywinks?
Changes. Canteen a coat of paint. Maurice a new suit. Boys cheekier. Girls' dresses.
Wish I was 40 years older.
Going to miss you. Compensations.
Family/grandchildren/marrow prize.
Free buses/hair cuts/cinema/shout at Bob.
R. C. Sheriff. When a man retires and time is no longer a matter of urgent importance, his colleagues generally present him with a clock.
30 years of sterling service should be recognized.

Notes

A retirement presentation should not, perhaps, be the occasion for a comic speech as such, since the occasion will inevitably be an emotional and to some extent a sad one – sometimes almost a tragic one, if the retiring person has no family. But a few mild jokes are *de rigeur* on these occasions, and should reflect the foibles, habits and little weaknesses of the retiree. If there isn't a lot to be said, i.e. if the person concerned is a rather nebulous, colourless character, you will just have to expand the customary sentiments about popularity, sense of humour, likeableness, helpfulness, value to the firm, etc., etc. Do not forget that your speech should be for the *retiring person*; he or she is the one you must try to please and impress, and if you achieve this everyone else present will be touched and satisfied.

1. Clean the windows – I have imagined here that Bill is well-known for his obsession with clean windows. If he is renowned for an appallingly untuneful voice, you can say, 'He really wanted to sing at Covent Garden . . . but all the porters complained.' Or, if his beer-drinking capacity is legendary, 'He wanted to be a water diviner but he kept finding something stronger'.

2. CB will be the name of a past managing director or famously tough supervisor. Tiddleywinks can be any ludicrous and fashionable pastime. As I write, skateboards are all the rage.

3. The marrow prize – most people have a hobby or an interest of some sort, and play can be made with Bill's known passion.

4. Bob can be the office junior, or someone known to irritate Bill, but keep the reference friendly, i.e. don't drag in the name of Bill's known arch enemy with whom he has been feuding childishly for 29 of the past 30 years.

Changes in the firm can be elaborated – take a little time out to check on the firm's history; this kind of information always goes down well in a speech, whether humorous or not, and it can be interlaced with 'do you remember, Bill?' which will probably prompt him to some humorous memory of his own. If the presentation is a cheque, you can say, 'I haven't deducted my commission, Bill – you can buy me a pint in the Club later. Now you can afford to buy a season ticket to Honest Alf's!' Honest Alf will be the local bookie, if Bill is known to be a gambling man.

Further material of possible use may be found in the Presentation Proposal speech on page 179.

36

Retirement: Reply

Thank you, so much, Martin, for that wonderful speech ...
a really wonderful speech ... of course, I've had to pay for
mine out of my pension ...

It was that great man, Abraham Lincoln, who said, 'My
father taught me to work; he did not teach me to love it.'
And so I must say to you that much as I have enjoyed your
company over the past 30 years and much as I have
appreciated all that the firm has meant to my family and
myself like most of us and like Abraham Lincoln I have
never really loved work, and so I have mixed feelings about
retiring as we all do about any change in our routines.

In fact when I first came here, the manager then, old Mr
Marley, said to me, 'Well, boy, do you like hard work?'
And I said, 'No, sir.' 'That's the first truthful answer I've
had all day – I'll take you on.' I worked first of all as the
lift boy – how I enjoyed that! But I got taken off that after
taking the Chairman down one day; the lift came to a rather
sharp stop and I said, 'Was that too fast for you, sir?' And
he said, 'No, Bill, I always wear my trousers round my
ankles[1] ...'

Mr Legree was still with us then – he was a hard man.
We had one old chap with us then, he went into Mr
Legree's office and asked for a day off. 'Why?' said Mr
Legree, 'you've had your holiday entitlement, haven't you.'
'Oh yes sir,' said the old chap, 'but it's my Golden Wedding
Anniversary and we've got our children and grandchildren
and relations coming from all over the world to see us, so
I'd be very grateful if you could let me have the day off,
sir.' 'Great Heavens,' said Mr Legree, 'have I got to put up
with this every fifty years ... ? !' ... Oh yes, things were
much tougher in those days [2] ...

When I started I got 35 shillings – that's one seventy-five
– for a 48-hour week. I only got ten days holiday a year –

and there weren't even so many Bank Holidays then. There was no clubroom, the canteen was a dirty, draughty Nissen Hut, the lavatories were outside, conditions in the plant were primitive to say the least . . . I must have been mad to come here [3] . . . but I'm very glad I stuck it out, because I've been very happy here . . . on the whole. The place has fed me and my family and paid the mortgage and provided me with some wonderful friends. So I leave you with the happiest of memories, a few regrets, and my sincerest thanks for this magnificent cheque (*or whatever*). Thank you, all of you.

Suggested Headings

Wonderful speech. Paid for mine out of pension.
Abe Lincoln. My father taught me to work; he did not teach me to love it.
Much as I've enjoyed your company/never really liked work.
Mr Marley. Like hard work? No, sir.
Worked as lift boy.
Mr Legree. Golden Wedding.
When I started 35s for 48hr week. 10 days holiday/not so many Bank Holidays. No club/canteen dirty and draughty Nissen Hut/ lavatories outside/conditions primitive. I must have been mad.
Been very happy/on the whole.
Place has fed me and family. Paid mortgage. Provided me with wonderful friends.
Leave with happiest of memories, a few regrets and thanks.

Notes

1. This is a sample story – any story of your early days with the firm, especially if it involves a long-departed legend-ary director or boss will go down well.
2. This paragraph is representative of the stories told about tough middle-management bosses and also about quaint old eccentrics of the past.

3. Horror stories of conditions in the bad old days are always popular, but don't seize the opportunity to talk union or party politics.

I read in the newspaper not so long ago of the worker whose retirement speech at his presentation was so abusive that he got himself and his firm into the headlines. 'I've hated every minute of it,' he said, 'and I'm glad I'm going.' This is one approach of course, but we are concerned with comic speeches in this book. Although I am quite prepared to concede that the spectacle of the managing director and senior executives gathered to honour one of their honest artisans who tells them just what he thinks of them is indeed rich in comedy. I feel that you wish to be less abrasive and more conventional. Try to do without notes – in this instance it looks so much better if you appear to speak spontaneously. Be ready to respond to the subject matter of the proposer's speech – and to your gift, if any. If you are returning in a part-time capacity or are remaining as an officer of any of the staff associations or clubs you can refer to this – 'Anyhow, you don't get rid of me that easily because I shall still be playing the tuba in the works band. I remember the last concert we played. Geoff said to me after one number, 'What's the next, then?' I said, 'The British Grenadiers.' He said, 'What – again? I've just played that ... !'

The following might be of use:
I was late to work and my boss said to me, 'Why are you late?' I said. 'My Mum's just had a baby.' He said, 'Well, all right, but don't let it happen again.' I said, 'That's what me Dad said ...'

The manager said to me once, 'There's only one honest way to make a living. Do you know what it is?' I said, 'No, sir.' He said, 'No, I thought you wouldn't.'

37

Stag Night: Proposal

Welcome to the wake, gentlemen . . . yes, it's another good man gone . . . another good man lost to the warm, fragrant, soft, pliant, earthy, passionate, fleshy charms of . . . whoops, nearly got myself going here . . . down, boy, down . . . of course, some girls shrink from making love . . . others get bigger and bigger [1] . . .

Here you are then, Jack, your last night of freedom . . . just think of your little Julie getting her torso ready – trousseau ready . . . She's a cracker, though, isn't she, eh? Not like some of the dogs you've had in your time. There was that Hazel – she had beautiful eyes – especially the middle one . . . but she was so ugly! When she walked in the kitchen all the mice jumped on the chairs. She had long blonde hair all down her back . . . none on her head, just all down her back . . . I remember saying to her once, when old Jack was out the back having a quick whatsit, 'Do you smoke after you've made love?' She said, 'I dunno – I never looked . . .' Do you remember her, Jack? You used to call her Treasure 'cos she had a big chest . . . and she looked as though she'd been dug up . . .

Then there was Fat Freda – he first saw her on holiday at Torquay. She was swimming in the nude . . . in the sea as well, but in the nude . . . with a friend. Yes, her friend was breasting the waves and she was doing the opposite, so Jack waved back and one thing led to another . . . She was such a noisy eater. I remember once when my dolly of the day, Fat Freda and Jack and me made up a foursome. She'd just come from hospital after a cosmetic operation – they couldn't lift her face so they'd lowered her body . . . anyway, we went for dinner at Greasy Guiseppe's. When she started on the soup six couples got up and did the rumba . . .

After her came a little number we all used to call Angel

Delight, 'cos she was so easy to make . . . She was a nice-looking kid – at least her teeth were all her own. I know they were her own 'cos she showed me the receipt. She had Jack eating out of her hand, didn't she, Jack? Well, it saved the washing-up . . . but he wouldn't marry her, the swine. One night Jack and I were on the batter and we bumped into her – he'd stood her up, the cur! She burst into tears and said, 'I'll wind up an old maid!' And Jack said, 'Well, that's a funny way to spend an evening – I'd rather have another pint.' But when she left, he couldn't sleep – could you, Jack, eh? She'd taken the bed with her.

Then there was Margot, the one with airs and graces. Jack told me he took a bottle of champagne to her flat once – only once. He was pouring it out and he said, 'When?' And she said, 'As soon as I've had my champagne.' Fair enough . . . She was a dancer, wasn't she, Jack? With her left foot she did tap, with her right she did ballet . . . and in between the two she made a fortune . . . Mind you, she said she was faithful – faithful! Hah – she had corns on her shoulder blades.

But my favourite was the red-head – she used to keep it polished with nail-varnish – Muscles. We called her that 'cos she was in everyone's arms . . . She was a raving beauty – escaped from Colney Hatch.[2] She came from a very polite family though – ten girls and they all called their mother Madam . . . Everyone's very friendly there – I've still got the phone number if anyone's interested. If a man answers don't hang up, 'cos he's a lot of fun, too . . . Muscles – what a girl . . . when she died they buried her in a Y-shaped coffin . . .

So, Jack, you're finally doing it . . . you know Mr Punch's advice to those about to get married – don't. But you can quite understand how a chap would want to marry such a lovely and innocent creature as Julie . . . even the men's side of the laundry list is a complete mystery to her . . . Do you know how they first met? Julie was wearing a very short skirt at the bus stop, Jack was next in the queue . . . doing up his shoelaces . . . Julie looked down at him and said, 'You're no gentleman.' He said, 'I can see you're not . . .'

The last time I was at a wedding the couple didn't hit it off. Right from the start there was trouble. He had one of those Polaroid cameras, and he took a picture of his bride in the nude, in their hotel room. Then she took one of him in the same condition . . . but she looked at the photo and shook her head. He said, 'What's wrong with it?' She said, 'I'll have to get it enlarged . . .' She was a quick thinker that girl, though. One evening when her husband came home unexpectedly he found a naked man in the wardrobe. She said, 'Don't get excited – he's a nudist come in to use the phone . . .'

Then one night he was doing his exercises on the bedroom floor. He was just doing his press-ups when she said, 'Why don't you get into bed and kill two birds with one stone . . . ?' She was doing the ironing one night and moaning on about woman's work never being done – you'll find out, Jack – and he said, 'Well, you needn't iron that bra for a start – you've got nothing to put in it.' She said, 'Well, I iron your underpants, don't I . . . ?' But the last straw came when they were in bed one night and she said, 'I've got a confession to make. I've been to bed with another man.' He said, 'So have I – turn over . . .'

But you must take this marriage business seriously, Jack. I remember when I got married – it was a quiet family affair, just me, the wife and the kids . . . Her mother couldn't be there – she was away on manoeuvres at the time . . . I said to the vicar, 'Do you believe in sex before the wedding?' He said. 'Not if it delays the ceremony . . .' He said to me, 'Now look here, I never had improper relations with my wife before we were married. Have you?' I said, 'I dunno – what was her maiden name . . .'

I'll never forget our honeymoon . . . God knows I've tried . . . There we were, lying in bed with the moonlight streaming in through the holes in the roof. The wife cuddled up to me and said, 'Here, mister . . . (We hadn't known each other all that long.) She said, 'Will you love me when I'm old and ugly?' I said, 'Darling, of course I do . . .' She said, 'Will you love me in the hereafter . . . ?' I said, 'If I don't get what I'm here after you'll be here after I've gone . . . !'

And you must protect your wife, Jack. Protect her against insults. I was in the Bell the other night and there was this party of four at the next table – two couples – when suddenly one of the husbands . . . broke wind ! . . . He must have been on (*local brew*) . . . The other husband was furious. He said, 'How dare you break wind before my wife?' The fellow said, 'I'm terribly sorry – I didn't know it was her turn . . .'

You've got to be careful, too, if you're getting married. As I came in here tonight a chap came staggering up to me and said, 'Did you sleep with my wife last night?' I said, 'No . . . not a wink . . .' I think it must have been (*whoever*).

Anyway, Jack, it's better to marry than burn, so they say – and you know what happened to the over-sexed squirrel, don't you? . . . did his nut . . . We're sure that you've made a wise decision and may the future give you all you want yourself. Good luck tomorrow, and here's to you!

Suggested Headings

Another good man lost to the warm, fragrant, soft, pliant, earthy, passionate, fleshy charms.

Some girls shrink from making love.

Last night of freedom. Julie getting her torso – trousseau ready.

Hazel. Beautiful eyes, especially middle one.

Ugly – mice jumped on chairs. Long blonde hair all down her back. Smoke after making love? Treasure – big chest and dug up.

Fat Freda. Swimming in the nude with friend. Breasting the waves. Cosmetic op – couldn't lift face so lowered her body.

Noisy eater – six couples got up and did rumba.

Angel Delight. Easy to make. Nice-looking/teeth all her own.

Had Jack eating out of her hand. I'll wind up an old maid. When she left Jack couldn't sleep.

Margot. Bottle of champagne. When? As soon as I've had my champagne. L foot tap/R foot ballet. Faithful – corns on shoulder blades.

Red-head/nail-varnish/Muscles. Raving Beauty/Colney Hatch.

Polite family/10 girls all called their mother Madam. Still got number/if man answers. Y-shaped coffin.

So Jack, you're finally doing it.

Mr Punch's advice.

Lovely innocent creature as Julie. Men's side of laundry list.

Met at bus stop. You're no gent. Last wedding. Couple didn't hit it off. Polaroid camera. Have to get it enlarged.

Naked man in wardrobe. Nudist come in to use the phone.

Press-ups. Why not get into bed and kill two birds.

Ironing bra. Nothing to put in it.

Wife. Been to bed with another man.

Take marriage seriously. My wedding quiet family affair. Mother-in-law on manoeuvres. Said to vicar: Do you believe in sex before the wedding? Vicar. Never had improper relations with my wife. Have you?

My honeymoon. Moonlight through holes in roof. Here mister.

Old and ugly. Hereafter.

Protect your wife.

Two couples in Bell. How dare you break wind before my wife?

Did you sleep with my wife last night?

Better to marry than burn. Over-sexed squirrel?

May the future give you all you want yourself.

Notes

1. Or: some girls fight against making love, others take it lying down.
2. Colney Hatch – lunatic asylum.

This occasion is traditionally marked by excessive boisterousness, alcoholic intake and blue stories – not necessarily in that order. I have indicated the less obscene stories of the kind which might be thought suitable. The speech given here is of course much too long, but then if you don't get your oration in fairly early in the evening no-one will want to listen to more than a couple of sentences anyway. So if you've been asked to perform, do it sooner than later.

The speech is unashamedly a string of gags loosely strung together round the theme of marriage, and presented by a cod run-down of Jack's past flames. How long you should stay on your feet is something you can only judge at the time. Be prepared either to expand or to cut; mark your notes accordingly. As to how blue you can get depends on whether the party is held in a public place or not. My publisher's fastidiousness rules out samples of really blue stag material, but I would recommend you to try and obtain a copy of G. Legman's 'Rationale of the Dirty Joke' (Panther). Series 1, which is in two volumes, is difficult to find but devotees of the genre will find it a fascinating work. Series 2 I have not seen but would seem to be more of the same.

My Collins' Graphic English Dictionary defines 'stag' amongst other things, as 'The male of the bovine genus castrated at such an age that he never gains full size' . . .

Finally, before the evening starts: drink half a pint of milk . . .

38

Stag Night: Reply

Thank you, Malcolm – who writes your jokes, Tchekov? [1]
As I look round I am reminded of Oscar Wilde . . . if the
cap fits, Ronnie . . . who said – amongst many other things
– that 'work is the curse of the drinking classes' . . . Let's
all drink to that.

Well, now, as winner of the Shoreham-by-Sea Errol
Flynn Appreciation Society 19— Silver Screw Award for
Keeping Women in Their Proper Place,[2] I feel that I have
the right to tell all you bachelors that it's all very well for
you to scoff and jeer at a chap about to get married. You
may think that there are plenty more fish in the sea, but one
day you may wake up and find that your bait's gone
stale . . .

Yes, tomorrow's the big day. I went to the doctor last
week for a check-up . . . Well, it's only fair, isn't it? I mean
I don't want my bride catching a – cold or anything, do I?
When I went in I saw that the doctor had this rectal thermometer sticking out of his breast pocket. So I said, 'What
have you got a rectal thermometer in your pocket for,
doctor?' He looked down and said, 'Oh, blast – that means
some bum's got my fountain pen . . .'

Do you know how Julie and I met? It was at a party at
Sarah's, and she said to me – Julie, that is – 'If you catch
me you can kiss me and if you can't catch me I'll be behind
the sofa' . . . No, it's not true, not true . . . it was in the
cupboard under the stairs . . . Her mother's a wonderful
woman – she'll be there tomorrow, of course – they're
giving her a 24-hour parole . . .

I hope things won't change all that much after the
wedding – Charlie and I will still be on the terraces every
Saturday to support the greatest football team in the
country – Scunthorpe United.[3] The last time we went the
ground was packed and half way through the first half I

got caught short – remember, Charlie? So I said 'What can I do? I'll never get through this lot'. So Charlie said, 'Do it in that chap's wellies.' I said, 'I can't – he'd notice.' Charlie said, '*You* didn't . . .'

Julie and I will also be keeping our usual Friday visit to the Palais – we did some serious courting in the car park outside the Palais. This policeman used to come round shining his torch in the parked cars after chucking-out time – well, he had to get his kicks somehow, I suppose – and he stopped at one car peering in for a long time, goggle-eyed. Eventually the window was wound down and the girl inside said, 'Yes?' He said, 'What are you up to?' She said, 'Oh, we're just practising the paso doble.' He went on to the next car, peered in through the window then tapped on the glass. The girl inside said, 'Yes?' he said. 'What are you doing?' She said, 'We're doing the cha-cha-cha.' At the third car when the girl wound down the window he said, 'I suppose you're doing the bossa nova?' She said, 'No, I'm doing the boss a favour . . .'

I believe a couple should keep little secrets to themselves, just to maintain an element of mystery, of spice. There was this couple I used to know, been married for years, and one day when an American Rodeo was touring round the husband astounded his wife by saying that he would enter for the bucking bronco competition – £1,000 for anyone who could stay on the bucking bronco for three minutes. His wife went spare! 'What do you know about bucking broncos?' she said. 'You've never been on a bucking horse in your life!' He said, 'You don't know everything about me. If I say I can ride a bucking bronco then I'll ride the bucking thing!' And he did! To his wife's amazement, he stayed on that bucking fierce mount for fifteen whole minutes! The crowd went mad, and of course he got his £1,000. His wife was aglow with pride and admiration for this totally unexpected talent of her husband's, and she said to him, 'But darling, where did you learn to ride a bucking bronco?' He said, 'Well, you remember the time you had whooping cough . . .'

Well, fellas, I'd better sit down before I fall down. Just

208

before I do I have one further little story – but I need a bit of help because I've been up all day . . . if you'll pardon the expression . . . and I've had a skinful, so will you help me? . . . Right, well, this story concerns three little ducks called (*hold up one finger*) Quack, (*hold up two fingers*) Quack-Quack, and (*hold up three fingers and let the company say 'Quack-Quack-Quack'*) – ooh, you *are* quick! Shall we try that again? Three little ducks called (*one finger*), (*two fingers*) and (*three fingers*) lived in the country, and one day they decided to collect some mushrooms. So out they went with a great big basket, did (*one finger*), (*two fingers*) and (*three fingers*) and they filled that basket to the brim, went home, made themselves a pot of delicious mushroom soup and drank it all to the last drop, and it was absolutely scrumptious. But – in the middle of the night (*one finger*) fell ill . . . aaaah! . . . so (*two fingers*) said to (*three fingers*) 'You'd better go for the doctor.' So he did, the doctor came, examined (*one finger*) and said, 'Oh, he'll be all right, he's just got a touch of indigestion. Give him these pills and he'll be fit again by the morning.' But, by the time morning came – (*one finger*) had died! . . . aaah . . . whereupon (*two fingers*) said to (*three fingers*) 'I think that doctor must have been a bit of a (*one finger*).' Thank you.

Suggested Headings

Who writes jokes/Tchekov?

Oscar Wilde: work is the curse of the drinking classes.

Shoreham-by-Sea Errol Flynn App Soc 19— Silver Screw for Keeping Women in Their Proper Place.

More fish in the sea – bait's gone stale.

Saw doctor for check up. Rectal thermometer. Some bum's got my fountain pen.

How Julie and I met. Party at Sarah's. Catch me behind the sofa.

Things won't change. Charlie and I still support Scunthorpe United.

Caught short. Wellies.

Julie and I usual Friday visit to Palais.

Car park. Policeman shining torch in parked cars. Paso doble.
Cha-cha-cha. Bossa nova.
Couple should keep little secrets. Bucking bronco. Whooping cough.
Sit down before I fall down.
Three little ducks.

Notes

1. Tchekov can be altered to any prominent boring person – a politician or ubiquitous TV personality.
2. This award can be altered to whatever you feel is appropriate to your particular part of the country and known attitude to the gentler sex.
3. Scunthorpe United will be a local team renowned for being the worst in the local league. If you are known not to be a football fan this story can be altered to a queue for a rock concert, or any suitable event.

Like the previous speech, this is a thinly disguised catalogue of ruderies, except for the final joke which is just a silly bit of nonsense – the company will be drunk enough by the time you get to speak to go along with the childishness of it. Good luck, my son.

39

The Stage

Oh – is that me? . . . I'm so sorry, I'm a little hard of hearing – all that applause, you know. Accustomed as I am to public speaking . . . I am more than a little diffident about addressing so distinguished, intelligent (*putting spectacles on*) and good-looking an audience (*look at audience and blanch, then remove spectacles hurriedly*). That was a mistake . . . Can you hear me all right? I only ask because I've just finished at the National . . . boy, am I finished at the National . . . We had a lot of complaints about acoustics, so dear Larry and that nice Peter Hall spent a whole afternoon putting down traps and poison [1] . . .

The theatre tradition is very strong in my family. I was born in the theatre – it went over so big my mother kept it in the act. One of my ancestors played with Kean – he was the little boy next door . . . My mother was such a graceful slip of a girl – she did an act on the Halls. She would bend over backwards and pick up a handkerchief in her teeth. And then, to roars of applause, she would bend over backwards – and pick up her teeth. Dad was mostly in musical comedy, but his last show, a tour of 'Good Night, Vienna', came to an abrupt end in Walthamstow – well, if you lived in Vienna would you go and see 'Good Night, Walthamstow'? [2]

One of my aunts has just finished a film. She'll be getting the prints from Boots on Friday. My uncle Bill used to work in a circus mucking out elephants. My father said to him once, 'Why don't you pack that in and get yourself a decent job?' He said, 'What – and give up show business . . . ?' My grandfather was a marvellous old actor, but he went to the bad and finished up being condemned for murder. He stood on the scaffold and the prison governor said to him, 'Have you any last words?' Grandad, a true pro to the last, said (*looking down and stamping*) 'Yes – is this rostrum safe [3] ... ?'

Not that I was all that keen on the stage as a career when I was a child – I wanted to be a butcher so's I could get my own back on the ham – but then I won the National Talent Contest for the Sons of Indigent Bachelors.[4] It was a sweet little act – I was the original Jimmy Porter on the Slack Wire [5] ... Then I was fired with this great ambition to be legitimate – we all have it from time to time, I suppose – so I auditioned for RADA and got a place. What an audition! I gave 'em fourteen sonnets and the cigar boxes (*mime the boxes*),[6] a solo version of Act Two of 'Man and Superman' and the big boots ... and a yard and a half of Racine with the plate-spinning. I did well at RADA: in my last year I won the coveted Kenneth Griffiths Brass Spittoon for Not Going Over The Top.

My first professional engagement was with Harry Hanson's twice-nightly tatters at the Abattoir, Aberystwyth – not a bad date. Running water on every floor – 'course, it did make the dog-ends soggy but when you're young ... Then I was engaged for my first Christmas show. It was a Jewish pantomime – 'Abe's In The Wood.' Laugh! ... I thought they'd never start ... This was in Bradford, famous in theatrical history as the town where Irving died ... some of those clubs can be murder ... Still, the critics loved me – always a dangerous sign. You know what a critic is, don't you? Someone who leaves no turn unstoned.

Then I went to the open-air theatre in Regent's Park. I won't say anything about the standard of the company but at the first dress rehearsal six trees walked out. After the rehearsal the director said, 'Now then, gentlemen, this is an Elizabethan piece and you are all therefore in tights. Will you please wear your jock-straps in future?' And a little voice from the back said, 'Does that apply to the small parts as well [7] ... ?'

So that's how my career started, and since then I've done everything except incest and folk-dancing – any offers? I've been on television, of course. I was on it only last night – When I'm drunk I'll sleep anywhere ... I have a set in every room in the house . . . well, nearly every room . . . I mean, you must have somewhere to go when Russell Harty's on, mustn't you [8] . . . ? But I must admit that a great deal of television is rubbish – in fact I'm told that the shortage of programme material is so acute that now they're scraping the top of the barrel. Then there is commercial radio, of which it has been so truly said that for the actor it has opened up a whole new field of unemployment . . .

But the business has given me many happy days . . . and busy nights . . . and I wouldn't have missed a moment of it. I've got my room booked in Denville Hall for my retirement. Last time I went there to visit some chums there were these three old actresses talking about which great historical figure they would like to have been. One said, 'I'd like to have been Mrs Siddons – wealth, respect, the greatest tragic actress in our history – and immortalized by Gainsborough.' The second said, 'I'd like to have been Ellen Terry – she was a very great actress, universally loved and admired. And beautiful with it.' The third said, 'I'd like to be Sarah Pippelini.' Rhet said 'Who?' She said, 'Sarah Pippelini – look, she's got top billing in this morning's paper.' The first old dear took the paper, looked at it and said, 'Oh, Maisie, you never could read a script – that's not Sarah Pippelini, it says, "Sahara pipeline laid by fifty men in four weeks"!'

Well, now, ladies and gentlemen, you're getting tired. Of course you can't please all of the people all of the time, and a wise man once said that the only way to entertain some people is to listen to them, so I am now about to listen – to you. Thank you.

Suggested Headings

Hard of hearing. All that applause.
Distinguished, intelligent, good-looking audience.
Finished at the National. Acoustics.
Born in the theatre.
Mother. Bent over backwards.
Dad. 'Good Night Vienna' in Walthamstow.

Aunt. Just finished a film. Boots.

Uncle Bill. Mucking out elephants.

Grandad : Murder. Is this rostrum safe?

I wanted to be a butcher.

Nat Talent Contest for Sons of Indigent Bachelors. Jimmy Porter on the Slack Wire.

Wanted to be legit so auditioned for RADA. 14 sonnets and cigar boxes. Solo version Act Two of 'Man and Superman' and big boots. Yard and a half of Racine and plate-spinning.

Won Kenneth Griffiths Spittoon for Not Going Over The Top.

First job. Harry Hanson's twice-nightly tatters at Abattoir, Aberystwyth.

Running water.

First Xmas show. Jewish pantomime : Abe's In The Wood. Laugh – thought they'd never start.

Bradford. Where Irving died. Some clubs can be murder.

Critics loved me. Someone who leaves no turn unstoned.

Open-air theatre at Regent's Park. First dress rehearsal six trees got up and walked out.

All gents wear jockstraps. Small parts.

Done everything except incest and folk-dancing.

TV. On it last night. Set in every room/except one/Russell Harty.

Programming rubbish. Scraping top of the barrel.

Commercial radio. New field of unemployment.

Profession has given me happy days/busy nights.

Denville Hall. Three old actresses. Mrs Siddons/Ellen Terry/Sarah Pippelini.

You're getting tired.

Can't please all of the people all of the time. Only way to entertain some is to listen.

Notes

1. If a new theatre or auditorium has opened near where you are speaking, alter this gag to incorporate it.
2. This is supposed to have been an actual remark made by

Jack Hylton, whose tour of 'Good Night, Vienna' had done very bad business in Walthamstow. When asked by a friend how the week had gone, he replied, 'About as well as you would expect "Good Night Walthamstow" to go in Vienna.'

3. Stories of your theatrical antecedents, true or false, can be extended indefinitely.

4. If you are female, make this 'Daughters of Deserving Spinsters.'

5. The original of this was an act called, 'The Chocolate Soldier on the Slack Wire'. Update the gag if you can think of a good alternative. But don't update too much if it is supposed to be an event from your childhood. (Jimmy Porter is 1956 vintage.)

6. The cigar boxes – this is the trick where a number of blocks of cigar-box shape and size are held by pressure on the two outer ones. Practise miming adding and/or subtracting.

7. If you can do a good authentic Robert Atkins impersonation so much the better.

8. Update Mr Harty unless he is still gracing the nation's screens.

If you are speaking to an audience of pros, none of the references in this speech will need explaining. If not it is probably better to cut rather than to expand to make them intelligible (and therefore ponderous) to the layman. Pros tend, when speaking about the business to get all maudlin about their 'duty to the public' and 'the show must go on' and their 'wonderful, loyal fans'. Put in some of this guff by all means if you think it is expected, but I am only concerned with the comic aspects of speaking on the subject and I have too much respect for my digestion to draft out any sample banalities for you.

The following might be of use:
'This scenery is extremely old, having been rather unfairly purloined from the great tragedian William Macready during one of his longer pauses . . .'

Two fifth-rate comics who had teamed up in a double act were stranded, penniless, in the north of England. They hadn't even the fare back to Brixton, so they were trudging back on foot when they found themselves walking along a canal bank as a long barge slowly slid past them. 'How about hitching a lift back to London on the barge?' said one. The other agreed and the bargee agreed to take them provided they worked for their passage. Nearing London they had to pass through a lock gate where the fees were based upon the cargo carried. 'What have you got aboard?' called out the lock-keeper. 'Fifteen tons of fertilizer and two comics,' said the bargee, at which one of the comics turned to the other and said, 'Aren't we *ever* going to get top billing . . . ?'

40

Visitors: Proposal

Ladies and gentlemen, before I introduce our visitors, I'd just like to tell you that our membership drive is doing extremely well – we've driven away 14 members in the past week alone . . . (*looking around*) Are you sure Ted Rogers started like this . . . ? No, things are really looking up for us in Worcester – I hear that next week they're sending us a missionary from Redditch. Oh, that reminds me – anyone here from Kidderminster? Your coach has gone [1] . . .

Well now, Dr Johnson once said, 'When a man knows that he is to be hanged in the morning, it concentrates his mind wonderfully.' So all last night I was concentrating my mind on what I would be saying to you this evening, but frankly nothing wonderful has emerged so far, other than to bid our visitors the warmest possible welcome and to tell you that in your honour the club bar is going to be extended to a length of no less than fifty yards! . . . (*cheers*) . . . of course, this will be very expensive so we can only afford one barmaid . . . (*groans*) . . . for each member! . . . (*cheers*) . . . there will be no pint pots . . . (*groans*) . . . only quarts! . . . and the beer will be diluted . . . (*groans*) with whisky! . . . (*cheers*) and the new closing time will be ten o'clock . . . (*groans*) . . . in the morning . . . ! (*cheers*).[2]

(*To visitors*) I'm sure you found that display of emotion deeply moving – I very nearly went . . .

(*At this point you will dilate upon your visitor's reputation, career, and value to society. Or not, as the case may be. See Guest of Honour proposal speech on page 115*).

. . . and so I have the honour and pleasure of asking you all to rise, and to drink the health of our most welcome and distinguished visitors, Mr and Mrs Henry Ballcock!

Suggested Headings

Membership drive. Ted Rogers.

Things looking up. Missionary from (*local*).

Anyone from (*local*)? Coach has gone.

Dr Johnson. When a man knows he is to be hanged in the morning, it concentrates his mind wonderfully.

Warmest possible welcome. In your honour bar is to be extended to 50 yds/only 1 barmaid/for each member/no pint pots/only quarts/beer diluted/with whisky/close at 10.00 in the morning.

Display deeply moving.

Career details.

All rise to drink the health of our most welcome and distinguished visitors, Mr and Mrs Henry Ballcock.

Notes

1. These place names will reflect local rivalries.
2. For insurance you can plant a few cheerers and groaners, just to get the thing going. If you have no club bar, say, 'In your honour there is shortly opening in the High Street – a new public house! . . . (*cheers*) . . . but it will only have one bar . . . (*groans*) . . . fifty yards long! . . . (*cheers*) . . . etc., etc.

If you are sure your visitor will not be offended, it always goes down well if you get the name slightly wrong. At a supper party of some sixteen pros I once had to make an impromptu speech thanking our guest of honour, that fine Scottish comedian, Stanley Baxter. Having very little time to think of anything to say, I referred to him as Mr Baldwin and later as Mr Baker – both misnomers being greeted with shrieks of laughter. Mind you, it was about three o'clock in the morning in an Armenian Restaurant in Edinburgh, which may have had something to do with the success of my little wheeze.

Jokes about your visitors' origins are compulsory in a comic speech of welcome, and the following may be of possible use:

Any town in Britain

I went there once. It was shut . . . (*As you say the name of the town, barely suppress a yawn, or a snigger . . .*)
I believe there is a football team or something there. I don't know much about it – at school I only played the Wall Game.

Australia

I can tell you're from Australia: you've still got the chain marks round your ankles.
Little boy: What's this picture? Teacher: That's a kangaroo, a native of Australia. Little boy: blimey – my sister married one of them!

France
Useful phrases

Pas de deux – father of twins.
Hors de combat – two tarts fighting.
Coq au vin – chicken on a lorry.
La petite chose – your flies are undone.

Germany

The only German I know is 'Ich liebe dich' . . . which roughly translated means 'I'm very fond of Richard' . . . or something like that . . .

India

Last time I went to India I took the wife and her mother. Ma-in-law liked it in India, 'cos she was sacred there.

Ireland

My old Dad came from Ireland. He used to dig for peat. Pete was his brother – he was always falling in the bog.

Islands

I went to the Canary Islands but I never saw a Canary. I

went to the Channel Islands but I never saw a Channel ...
wait for it ... then I went to the Virgin Islands ... never
saw a drop of rain the whole fortnight ...

Spain

The only Spanish words I know are 'mañana' which means
tomorrow and 'pyjama' which means tonight.

United States

From the revolting colonies ...

I am willing to love all mankind, except an American, *Dr
Johnson.*

A young American visitor to this country found himself in
a crowded railway compartment, in which the only spare
seat was taken by a snuffly, smelly, pampered little pekinese
dog. Very politely the young American asked the dog's
owner, a haughty looking dowager, if he could sit down.
He was completely ignored. Again he asked, 'May I sit
down, madame?' And again the dowager resolutely ignored
him. For a third time he asked for a seat, and for the third
time received not the courtesy of a reply. He thereupon
opened the train window, picked up the dog and hurled it
outside; then he shut the window and sat down in the
freezing silence which ensued. But then an Englishman in
the same compartment put down his *Times* and remarked,
'You know, you American chappies are strange. You drive
on the wrong side of the road, you eat with your fork in
the wrong hand, and now you've just thrown the wrong
bitch out of the window!'

An American couple visiting England had hired a car and
were driving through Somerset (*or local*) admiring the
scenery. They found they had lost track of the time, neither
had a watch, so they saw this old farmhand milking a cow
by the side of the road, and thought they would ask him.
The husband stopped the car and went over to the old boy
and asked him the time. The old fella lifted up ... the ...
er ... (*mime lifting udders until the audience gives the*

220

word to you) . . . and he said, (*stooping slightly as though squinting under the udders*) 'Arr, it be nigh on five o'clock, me deario.' The American said thank you and went back to his car, mystified. 'Hey, Muriel . . .' he said, 'this you gotta see. Go and ask that old codger for the time.' So Muriel went over, asked the old chap the time, and again he lifted up the . . . er . . . the . . . (*again wait for audience*) that's right . . . and said (*peering underneath*) 'It's just after five o'clock, me deario . . .' The husband said, 'Sir, that is fantastic. How do you do it?' And the old boy said, 'Well, if I do that (*miming lifting one udder*), it's no good, and if I do that (*miming lifting the other udder*) it's no good, but if I do *that* (*miming lifting both udders*) I can just see the clock tower down in the village yonder . . .'

I had a nasty experience once in the States. I was driving through Cheyenne territory when my car broke down. As I was walking to try and get help I became aware of being watched, of being not alone. As the sun rose I saw that I was totally surrounded by about a hundred Indians, all in their war paint. As I stood, they closed in on me, slowly but purposefully. Do you know what I did? There was nothing else for it – I bought a blanket.

California
A state which is washed on the west coast by the Pacific and cleaned on the east by Las Vegas.

Chicago
You're from the windy city . . . we had noticed.

Florida
A wonderful place to live, if you happen to be an orange.

Hawaii
I went to Hawaii once. At breakfast time I ate three grass skirts before I realized it wasn't shredded wheat .

221

New York
The City of Brotherly Shove.

Any Mid-West State
You must be from Pioneer stock. My family were tee-total as well.

Many of the States of the Union possess nicknames for their inhabitants. Visitors from these States will be delighted if you are able to mention them, as follows:

Alabama	Lizards
Arkansas	Toothpicks
California	Gold-hunters
Colorado	Rovers
Connecticut	Wooden nutmegs
Delaware	Musk rats
Florida	Fly-up-the-creeks
Georgia	Buzzards
Illinois	Suckers
Indiana	Hoosiers
Iowa	Hawk-eyes
Kansas	Jay-hawkers
Kentucky	Corn-crackers
Louisiana	Creoles
Maine	Foxes
Maryland	Craw-thumpers
Michigan	Wolverines
Minnesota	Gophers
Mississippi	Tadpoles
Missouri	Pukes
Nebraska	Bug-eaters
Nevada	Sage-hens
New Hampshire	Granite-boys
New Jersey	Blues *or* clam catchers
New York	Knickerbockers
North Carolina	Tar-boilers *or* Tuckoes
Ohio	Buck-eyes
Oregon	Web-feet *or* hard cases

Pennsylvania	Pennamites *or* leatherheads
Rhode Island	Gun flints
South Carolina	Weasels
Tennessee	Whelps
Texas	Beef-heads
Vermont	Green-mountain boys
Virginia	Beadies
Wisconsin	Badgers

All purpose rhyme:
> *You can always tell the Irish,*
> *You can always tell the Dutch;*
> *You can always tell the* (whatever),
> *But you cannot tell him much!*

The following story can be adapted to suit most locations:

I once met a young lady from the same town as our guest, and I was surprised to discover that she had a small but very sharp knife tucked in her garter . . . yes, I found that out . . . Anyway, I asked her what it was for. She said, to defend her honour. I said, 'Well, if you're going to stay in (*local*) you'll need a set of carvers!'

41

Visitors: Reply

Mr Chairman, thank you for your welcome, which was
most cordial, and thank you for your cordial, which was
even more welcome . . . It's very good of you to say how
glad you are to see me, but I think you should know that
no (*give occupation or nationality*) would ever turn down
the chance of a free meal. Even so, I'm very flattered that
so many of you are here today – mind you, I know very
well that if I were going to be hanged there'd be ten times
as many . . .

It's such a marvellous big place you have here, Mr Chairman. I understand that from next year instead of having a
Chairman you're going to elect a mayor . . . But in all
seriousness, it is indeed a great honour to be entertained
by the (*reading from paper*) Chipping Norton Combined
Spot-Welders, Midden Cleaners and Abattoir Operatives
Association – oh, no, that was last night . . . (*turn over
paper and give correct name of group you are addressing*)
. . . yes, it's a great honour. If my old headmaster could see
me now . . . he'd turn in his gymslip. Well, it was a very
progressive school, and comprehensive to a degree which
bordered on the exotic. A bit like (*local school*) only without the Family Planning Clinic . . .

The odd thing is I knew I'd be coming here today, because my father saw it in the future. A remarkable man,
he's only got one eye . . . he's got a glass eye and a crystal
ball . . . and he told me that I would be coming here today
before I knew myself! I said to him, 'How do you know?'
He said, 'I took the phone call . . .'

But it's my first visit to your . . . town . . . so I thought
I'd arrive early and see the sights; you know, have a stroll
around. Well, that took all of . . . must have been . . . oh . . .
four minutes at least . . . so I was walking down the High
Street watching the road sweepers hard at work [1] . . . when

this chap came up to me – he did look a mess! Unshaven, filthy dirty, clothes in rags – I think he was a refugee from (*local district*) and he said, 'Give us fifty pence for a bed, guv'nor.' I said, 'Well, I'd want to see it first . . .' He said. 'No, I want some money.' I said, 'What for?' He said, 'I haven't had a bite all day.' So I bit him . . .

Then I saw a strange sight – you do see some funny people walking about round here, though, don't you? I suppose it must be all those tourists [2] . . . and I saw this chap with a scrubbing-brush on the end of a piece of string. I thought, 'Well, I'll humour him, so I said, 'Nice dog you've got there . . .' He said, 'That isn't a dog, it's a scrubbing-brush on the end of a piece of string.' [3] I said, 'Oh, I'm terribly sorry. I thought you were a bit doolally.' As I walked away he looked down at the scrubbing-brush and said, 'That fooled him, didn't it, Rover . . . ?!'

I'd tell you more jokes but you'd only laugh . . .

I thought I'd have a pub lunch so I went to the (*local*). Did you know Charlie's gone topless? Yes! I had a beautiful girl serving me . . . for lunch, that is . . . lovely girl, big, you know . . . I've heard of waitresses getting their thumb in the soup but this was ridiculous . . . I did notice something odd about her, though – she was wearing half a bra! Just one cup! So I said to Charlie (*or real name*) – he's not been too well lately, by the way, he's suffering from an in-growing wallet – I said to him, 'What's the idea of that girl showing just the one?' He said, 'Oh, she's only part time . . .'

After lunch I saw a strange thing in the Centre. I was standing by the taxi rank when this flying saucer landed and out stepped this alien from outer space. He went up to the head of the rank and said to the taxi driver, 'Take me to your leader.' The driver said, 'Sorry, mate, I'm just going off [4] . . .' Well, that quite shook me as you may imagine, so I went for a nice quiet cup of tea at the Kozee Korner Kaff,[5] dainty teas. It was nice – I had some genuine rock cakes made with real local – limestone . . .

It was about time to make my way here, but I got lost. So I stood at this crossroads wondering which way to turn when a chap came walking past, just an ordinary chap out walking his gorilla, and I said to him, 'Can you tell me, does this road go to (*wherever*)?' He said, 'I dunno,' I said, 'Well, where does that one go to?' He said, 'I dunno.' I said, 'What about that one?' 'I dunno.' 'And that one?' 'Dunno.' I said, 'You don't know much, do you?' He said, 'I'm not lost . . .'

Just then a perfumed, bangled, naked arm snaked out of a doorway and curled itself round my neck . . . no, it wasn't the Chief Constable,[6] it was a woman! She said, 'I'll show you the way' . . . and she did . . . ! That was a bit naughty, wasn't it? Mind you, she didn't charge me . . . and it was so exciting! Well, I haven't ridden pillion on a push-bike for years . . .

So I arrived here more or less unscathed and I was in the washroom when I got buttonholed by the club drunk. I could tell he was the club drunk 'coz his zip was rusty. He said to me, 'Is this a pleasure trip or have you got the wife with you?' I said to him, 'Don't be rude about my missus, Phi – sir [7] . . . in any case you're drunk.' And he said to me, 'And you're ugly!' I said to him, 'You're pie-eyed . . . !' He said, 'Yes, but in the morning I'll be sober . . .'

It has truly been said that a visit is an endurance test of companionship, and I believe that I have delighted you long enough, so I will just finish by thanking you once again most sincerely on behalf of (*whoever*) and myself. Keep smiling – and don't let the blighters [8] get you down.

Suggested Headings

Welcome / cordial.
No (*whatever*) would turn down chance of a free meal.
Flattered at turnout. Hanged.
Marvellous big place. Elect a mayor.
Great honour be to entertained by Chipping Norton Spot-Welders, Midden Cleaners and Abattoir Ops.
Old headmaster. Gymslip. Comprehensive.
Like (*local school*) without Family Planning Clinic.

Father foresaw this visit. Clairvoyant – glass eye and crystal ball.

Took phone call.

First visit. Stroll to see sights. Four minutes.

High St watching road sweepers.

Chap unshaven filthy ragged. Refugee from (*local*). 50p for a bed. Haven't had a bite.

Funny people here. Tourists. Scrubbing-brush on the end of string. Tell you more jokes.

Pub lunch at (*local*). Topless. Thumb in soup. Half a bra.

Charlie – ingrowing wallet – part-time.

Centre. Alien from flying saucer to taxi driver.

Cup of tea at (*local*). Rock cakes.

At crossroads. Lost/chap walking gorilla/I'm not lost.

Naked arm from doorway. Not Chief Constable. I'll show you the way. Pillion.

Washroom here. Club drunk/rusty zip/pleasure trip or wife?

Drunk – ugly.

Visit is an endurance test of companionship.

Don't let the blighters get you down.

Notes

1. This should be a reference to some local controversy, i.e. shortage of road-sweepers. An alternative might be 'watching the traffic swerve round the holes in the road . . .'
2. This only makes sense if you are speaking in an obviously non-tourist town, i.e. Bolton or Wolverhampton. Otherwise alter it to refer to a local firm ('all those fitters from the depot') or institution ('all those planners from the Town Hall').
3. Use the local accent if you can make a good stab at it.
4. The same.
5. This should be some notorious coffee bar where the very idea of anything 'dainty' is ridiculous.
6. This should be any local well known character – manager of the football team, for instance, or the MP. Don't pick

anyone who might regard this crack as an offensive insinuation of homosexuality.
7. Here you can almost say the name of the club drunk, a name which will be recognized by everyone. It will of course be a man noted for his sobriety.
8. 'Blighters' can be a stronger word, if the occasion suits.

Further ideas may be gleaned from the Guest of Honour reply speech on page 119.

42

Wedding: Best Man

Now we come to the moment you've all been waiting for –
my speech . . . I have the honour of replying on behalf of
the bridesmaids and to thank you, sir, for your kind words.
They do all look lovely, don't they? Aren't those dresses
wonderful? They'll be in *Exchange and Mart* next week
. . . but what about *my* gear then, eh? . . . the Ascot rig . . .
I'm breaking it in for Prince Philip . . .

Now, ladies and gentlemen, a lot of nonsense is spoken
about marriage, and no doubt I will be adding to it . . . but
I think marriage is a bit like a tourniquet – they both stop
circulation. Still, it is said that matches are made in heaven
. . . apart from those that come from Sweden . . . but wherever they come from, Tom and Vera, you have married
each other now for better of for worse. Tom certainly
married for better, and Vera . . . well, Tom, when she starts
wrapping your sandwiches in a road map you'll know it's
time to kiss and make up. Or something.

When she was a little girl – her Mum told me this – Vera
was passionately devoted to horses [1] – passionately! Which
prompts us to take another very close look at Tom . . . but a
funny thing happened outside the church after the photo-
graphs were taken. Here was this little girl standing there
– she'd just happened to be passing by – so I said to her,
'Wasn't the bride lovely?' And she said, 'Yes, but she
changed her mind quickly.' I said, 'What do you mean?'
She said, 'Well, she went in the church with one man and
came out with another!' . . . I said to her, 'Are you going to
get married some day?' She said, 'Yes. I'm going to marry
the boy next door.' I said, 'That's nice.' She said, 'Well, I've
got to – I'm not allowed to cross the road.'

Tom and Vera will be very happy, I'm sure. They're the
right ages for each other for a start – I think a big disparity
in ages can be a problem, don't you? I read in the paper

only the other day of a girl of 18 – only 18 – who married an old boy of 82 . . . Now she know's what it's like to have old age creeping up on her . . . Then there were the Welsh couple – their marriage was nothing but rows. Well, she was Presbyterian and he was Sunday opening . . .

Tom and Vera will shortly be off on their honeymoon, somewhere romantic and quiet and beautiful and sunny. I must confess I don't think I would have chosen Scunthorpe (*or local*) but then . . . at least this time of the year the sheets are still clean. I'll never forget my first night of connubial bliss. There were two embroidered texts on the wall over the bed. On my wife's side it said, 'I Need Thee Every Hour' . . . and on my side it said, 'Lord, Give Me Strength.' We didn't stay long [2] . . .

Of course, I've known Tom for ten years now, and in all that time he's always proved himself to be . . . er . . . he's a very good . . . er . . . everyone says he . . . er . . . what I mean is . . . er . . . been a funny sort of day, hasn't it [3] . . . ?

One word of advice, Tom: the problem all newly married men have to come to terms with – what do you call your mother-in-law? Well, why don't you do what I did – for the first year I just said, 'Oi – you!' and after that I called her Gran.

Once again I thank you on behalf of the bridesmaids. May they all very soon be taking Shakespeare's advice to 'go down on their knees, fasting, for a good man's love' . . .

(*After which you will either introduce the next speaker, if any, or begin the reading of the letters and telegrams.*)

Suggested Headings

Moment you've all been waiting for.

Honour of replying on behalf of the bridesmaids. Look lovely.

Dresses wonderful. *Exchange & Mart.*

My gear? Ascot rig. Breaking it in for Prince Philip.

Nonsense spoken about marriage. Like a tourniquet.

Matches are made in heaven.

Tom and Vera married for better or for worse.

Tom. Wrapping up your sandwiches in a road map.

Vera passionately devoted to horses.

Little girl outside. Bride changed her mind. In with one man out with another. Marry the boy next door. Not allowed to cross the road.

Tom and Vera right ages. Girl of 18 married man of 82. Old age creeping up on her.

Welsh couple. She Presbyterian and he Sunday opening.

Honeymoon. Romantic and quiet and beautiful and sunny (*local*).

Sheets still clean.

My first night. Texts over bed. Wife's: *I Need Thee Every Hour*. Mine: *Lord, Give Me Strength*.

Known Tom for 10 years.

What do you call your mother-in-law?

Thanks again on behalf of bridesmaids: Shakespeare's advice to 'go down on their knees, fasting, for a good man's love.'

Notes

The best man's speech is traditionally a comic one; very often a desperate and nervous best man simply strings together a number of blue jokes which are either not especially funny or extremely embarrassing or both. (See 'Content' on page 13.)

1. Substitute any interest to which the bride may have had as a child – you may need to do a little prior detective work to discover something suitable.

2. If you are not married, this story can be attributed to the Welsh couple – 'She was Presbyterian and he was Sunday Opening . . . mind you, right from the start they were in trouble, those two. On the first night of the honeymoon there were two embroidered texts over their bed, etc, etc.'

3. If the weather is fine, alter this to 'Turned out nice again, hasn't it?' The point is that unable to think of anything nice to say about the groom, you fall back on a standard banality. If the room is your brother you could perhaps alter this entirely to a comic life history. (See Birthday

Party proposal on page 57. Coming of Age proposal on page 84 and the reply on page 90. Guest of honour proposal on page 115. Presentation proposal on page 179. Promotion proposal on page 187. Stag Night proposal on page 201).

The following stories and cracks may be of use:

The trouble with being the best man is that I'll never get the chance to prove it.

You can tell this is a love-match pure and simple – she's pure and he's – no!

I'm not married myself – I've always been round-shouldered.

I've been told it's time I took a wife myself, and I agree. The only question is – whose . . . ?

I can't help it if I'm not married – I was born that way.

Don't go mad with babies, remember there's a world food shortage.

43

Wedding Anniversary: Proposal

It was Dr Johnson who said: 'Marriage may bring pains but celibacy brings no pleasures,' and we are celebrating today the tenth anniversary of two people who had the wisdom to accept the good Doctor's advice. The tenth anniversary is of course a tin wedding which is only appropriate – Doris has fed him out of tins for years ... (*See list on page 237*).

There is always something joyful and heartening about the whole business of weddings and marriage – like the chap who went to the undertaker to bury his wife. The undertaker said, 'Haven't I seen you before, sir? Didn't I bury your wife two years or so ago?' The man said, 'Yes, but I married again.' And the undertaker said, 'Congratulations ... !'

You see, it's a reflex action, whenever we think of marriage and wedding anniversaries we go all soft and sentimental. And why not, eh, Sid? Look at him there – just because he isn't in the first rosy flush of flaming youth, that doesn't mean his pilot light's gone out, does it?

I don't know whether you know this, but every year, on their anniversary, Doris bakes a little cake. A special one, just for the two of them. And I know Sid has regarded these cakes as milestones ... marking their happy years together. Sid always likes to make an occasion of their anniversary. Last year he took Doris to see United [1] ... and this year he's bought her a 50-piece after-dinner set – a packet of toothpicks ...

There's one old couple living near us, they recently had their Golden Wedding and I was invited. Well, there was this Frenchman there – he was staying with one of the neighbours or something – and he didn't know what a Golden Wedding was all about. So I explained it to him, saying, 'The ... old homme and the old femme ... compris? (I speak it like a native, as you can tell . . . not much like a frog but just like a native . . .) Anyway – the old homme and the old femme avez lived together pour . . . fifty annies . . .' 'Ah,' he said, 'and now zey are getting married – bravo!'

This old couple – very touching, really – they decided to go off to their old honeymoon hotel for a few days, just to relive old times and old memories. So they arrived at the same hotel – they hadn't been back for fifty years – and they even managed to get the same room. Same bed . . . same sheets . . . same dirty cracks on the ceiling . . . somebody must have written 'em standing on a chair . . . They had dinner – the same as they'd had half a century before – a bottle of wine, a few liqueurs and up they tottered, just the same. The dear old couple, worn out with the travel and the emotional upheaval, lay there in bed, thinking, and the wife said to her husband, 'Do you remember, Ben, when we were here before – you nibbled my ear . . .' He said, 'Well, hang on – I'll just go and get my teeth.' Then she said, 'You were so mad for me that first night you wouldn't even let me get my stockings off.' He said, 'Don't worry, love. Tonight you'd have time to knit yourself a pair[2] . . . !'

But very touching, I think, is the story of the very rich man who had never married, and one day he happened to be in a post office where he saw all the old folks queueing up for the pensions. He was particularly struck by the sight of one dear old couple standing side by side. He thought to himself, 'They've been through all their lives together, and now here they are, both drawing their old-age pension together.'

So he went up to them, produced his card and asked whether they would like to spend a week's holiday on his estate. They agreed and so for a whole wonderful week the old people lived the life of Riley – servants to see to their every whim, superb meals any time they fancied, big colour telly, drinks and smokes and trips out and about in the chauffeur-driven limousine – they'd never had such a week in their lives. And it didn't cost them a sou.

The last night came, and their host was having a final brandy and cigar with the old chap, and he said, 'Well, have you enjoyed your stay here?' 'Oh, yes sir, it's been simply grand,' said the old chap. 'You and your staff here couldn't have been nicer or kinder. I can't thank you enough. There's just one thing . . . ?' 'Yes,' said the host, wondering what on earth the old boy could have to complain about. 'Who's that old boiler I've been sleeping with all week . . . ?'

Well, Sid and Doris, things have certainly changed since you first tied the knot. In those days you could go to the flicks, have a couple of drinks, and a slap-up meal and still have change out of forty quid . . . Yes, things have changed – in 19—Sid still had his hair and Doris had her bikini [3] . . . mind you, some things change for the better – Sid's handicap is down to eighteen and Doris's knitting is coming along a treat [4] . . .

(*Here you may mention any children of the marriage or any member of the family who may be permanently residing with the anniversary couple.*)

So – here's to you, Sid and Doris, and here's to middle age, when you're old enough to know better but still young enough to go on doing it. Sid and Doris!

Suggested Headings

Dr Johnson. Marriage may bring many pains but celibacy brings no pleasures.

10th – Tin.

Undertaker. Bury your wife two years ago? Married again. Congratulations.

First rosy flush of flaming youth doesn't mean his pilot light's gone out.

Doris bakes cake. Milestones.

Last year took Doris to see United. This year 50-piece after-dinner set; packet of toothpicks.

Old couple celebrating Golden Wedding. Frenchman: they get married – bravo!

Original honeymoon, same room. She: Nibbled my ear/

teeth not time to take off stockings. He: Knit yourself a pair.

Rich man sees dear old couple in post office. Who's that old boiler I've been sleeping with all week?

Things have changed. Flicks, drinks, meal – change from £40.

Sid still has hair and Doris her bikini.

Changes for the better. Sid's handicap/Doris's knitting. (*Children and family*).

Here's to middle-age, when you're old enough to know better but young enough to go on doing it.

Notes

1. This should refer to any pastime or interest of Sid's of which Doris is known to disapprove of at least to disfavour, i.e. breeding whippets or playing darts or rally driving or whatever.

2. If the couple celebrating the anniversary really are elderly it might be kinder to omit this sequence. But if they are very old, my experience is that they won't mind a bit.

3. Adjust accordingly – 'Sid still has his Vespa and Doris her waistline

4. These references should be to known failures, i.e., if Sid's golf is as bad as ever and Doris is known to hate knitting. Sid's singing abilities and Doris's pottery disasters are the kind of things to mention

All the children should be mentioned ('It's true that children brighten a home – they never switch the lights off') also any pets. If there are any members of the orginal wedding-party present – the bridesmaids, parents-in-law, siblings – they should be mentioned too. If there have been tragedies and hardships, do not omit any mention at all but do not dwell of them either, e.g. Like all of us, they have known good times and bad, great joy and darkest tragedy, but they are still here, still together and still sweethearts as we know they always will be . . .'

236

The following might be of possible use:

Mrs Patrick Campbell, the great Edwardian actress, said of marriage: 'It's the deep, deep peace of the double-bed after the hurly-burly of the chaise-longue.'

For her anniversary this year Sid's given Doris some jewellery he bought off a millionaire – his name was Woolworth.

The names of the anniversaries comes from the gifts traditionally considered suitable for each respective year:

First	Cotton
Second	Paper
Third	Leather
Fourth	Silk
Fifth	Wood
Sixth	Iron
Seventh	Wool
Eighth	Bronze
Ninth	Pottery
Tenth	Tin
Twelfth	Linen
Fifteenth	Crystal
Twentieth	China
Twenty-fifth	Silver
Thirtieth	Pearl or Ivory
Thirty-fifth	Coral
Fortieth	Ruby
Forty-fifth	Sapphire
Fiftieth	Gold
Fifty-fifth	Emerald
Sixtieth	Diamond
Seventy-fifth	Diamond

44

Wedding Anniversary: Reply

Thank you, Bob. Ladies and gentlemen, (*look at notes*) three vests, five shirts, one pair of pyjam . . . sorry . . . (*take off top note and crumple it up*) . . . Daren't put anything down for five minutes . . . now then, ah yes. Mozart said, 'We poor common people must take wives whom we love and who love us.' If it was good enough for old Wolfgang it was good enough for me – that's just what this poor and common man did. Mind you, it wasn't easy getting Doris to the altar – I was nearly eliminated in the semi-finals . . .

Ma was all against me at first, wasn't she, Doris? But she came round after I gave her that lovely chair for her birthday. Trouble was, Doris wouldn't let me plug it in. But we're fine now – she knows her place . . . it's when she comes over to our place that the trouble starts . . . Not that I mind her staying with us, except that she will use my razor. She would have been with us tonight only she's been refused bail.[1]

Success in marriage is not only finding the right person, it is being the right person. Doris and I have had a good run up to the present – in fact we're in injury time now. We had a very quiet wedding, as some of you may remember. The vicar had laryngitis – no! – there was just Doris and Jack [2] and me and the kids . . . Doris looked radiant. She was bride and sunny . . . I was wed and windy . . .

I remember going to the boss and asking for some time off for our honeymoon. He said, 'How long do you want?' I said, 'Well, what do you suggest, sir?' He said, 'I dunno – I haven't seen your girl' . . . anyway, we went to Bognor . . . (*leaning to Doris*) it was Bognor, wasn't it? Yes, well, the weather was very nice . . . I think. At least that's what it said in the papers . . .

Here, talking of papers, I checked up on the *Argus* edition of our wedding-day.

(Here you can give the headlines of the day, items of interest, the name of the Prime Minister, the doings of Royalty, etc. You could also read out what was on radio and/or TV that night, also what was showing at the local cinemas or theatres. The prices quoted in advertisements are always good for a laugh. Your local newspaper office will find the edition you require, or possibly your local reference library. The reference library will also have copies of Keesing's Contemporary Archives *which will give you world events of the time.*

The children have been a great joy to us. Children really are those little bonds which hold a marriage together by keeping the parents too busy to quarrel with each other. But so many kids are a trial these days – so often they ape their parents in spite of every effort to teach them good manners...

So anyway, here we are after X years still loving and still companionable – still friends. Only yesterday I came in from the pub just after chucking-out time – I'd gone there with some of the lads straight from work – and I said to Doris, 'Is my dinner hot?' Without batting an eye-lid she said, 'It should be – it's been on the fire since half-past six...'

No, only I'm kidding . . . she'll kill me when you've all gone . . . thanks for coming and helping in the commemoration. Next year it'll be X years – we shan't be holding a party – just two minutes silence . . . But now to give you a special treat. I'm going to sing to you . . . oh yes I am – you've drunk my beer so you can hear me sing . . . It's a lovely song very suitable for this occasion; it was written by Admiral Lord Nelson himself and it's called 'Please Don't Talk About Me – One Eye's Gone' . . .

(In the ensuing laugh and/or groan start 'My Old Dutch' *altering* 'forty years' *to* 'six long years' *or* 'nineteen' *years or whatever.*)

239

Suggested Headings

3 vests, 5 shirts, I pair of pyjamas.

Mozart : We poor common people must take wives whom we love and who love us.

Not easy. Nearly eliminated.

Ma against me. Gave her a chair. Doris wouldn't let me plug it in.

Will use my razor. Refused bail.

Success in marriage. Not only finding the right person/ being the right person.

Doris and I in injury time.

Quiet wedding. Vicar had laryngitis. Just Doris and Jack and me and the kids.

Doris bride and sunny. I was wed and windy.

Went to boss to ask for time off. How long?

Went to Bognor. Weather was nice.

Talking of papers : (*quotations*).

Children a great joy. Keep marriage together by keeping parents too busy to quarrel.

Kids ape parents in spite of every effort to teach them good manners.

After X years still loving and companionable.

Came in after chucking-out time. Supper still hot?

Only kidding. She'll kill me. Thanks for coming.

Next year X years. No party/2 minutes silence.

Going to sing. You've drunk my beer. Suitable for the occasion.

By Nelson. Please Don't Talk About Me, One Eye's Gone.

Notes

1. Alternatives : on the snow-clearing, on manoeuvres, helping the police with their enquiries, couldn't get time off from the oil-rig, was refused parole, broke her broom stick, on a trucking run to Turkey.

   If mother-in-law is amongst those present you may feel that this entire paragraph will need to be cut. And you'll almost certainly be right, although the electric chair gag is such a woofer and so patently ridiculous that you might consider keeping it. I once knew a man whose wife and mother-in-law were the quiestest and most inoffensive women imaginable; he also was basically very gentle and kind but he used to bombard his wife's mother with every old Music Hall gag you can think of – to her face. She never seemed to mind much, and her son-in-law was actually very fond of her; the fact that everybody knew this took the edge of any potential embarrassment . . . but it was still a curious way to demonstrate a relationship. I don't recommend this approach: I just record it.

2. Jack is the best man and need only be mentioned if he is present or was known to have been present by the company.

The quotations from the papers can be followed by recollections of any untoward incidents at the wedding – i.e. latecomers, Uncle Charlie disgracing himself, one of the bridesmaids being discovered in a closet with the photographer ('still in her powder blue – and it does crease so . . .'), the vicar falling flat on his face, the organ blowing up, etc., etc.

The following might be of possible use:
When Shirley was born Carl was very disappointed, because he wanted a brother. He told his pal from next door, Tim, what a swizz he thought it was and Tim said, 'well, if you don't want the baby, why not send it back?' And Carl said, 'no – we can't. We've already used it a week . . .'

When we were first wed Doris knew nothing about cooking – couldn't even boil the washing-up water without burning it. Our first week in our new home, and she went out into the kitchen to get some ice for our drinks. She was out there for *ages*, so eventually I went out to see what she was up to – and she was standing there crying. I said, 'What's up, my little honey-blossom . . . ?' (I said it was our first week). And she said, 'I dropped the ice cubes, so I put them into hot water to clean them and now I can't find them . . . !'

241

45

Welcome Home: Proposal

Welcome home, Stuart . . . were you homesick? Yes, of course you were – I know that's why you left, 'cos you were sick of home – no! As the poet says: 'Be it ever so humble, there's no place like home' . . . and Stuart's home is nothing if not humble – have you seen it? Strewth . . . it's a shack with nudie pix all over the walls and ceiling – a sort of rude hut . . .

But anyway, Stuart, it's nice to see your dear old face again, and speaking as one who's had the misfortune to buy you a lunch I know just how dear that old face can be . . .

There have been a few changes while you've been away. Prince Philip's paying a visit to the UK. Chelsea are top of the League. The pound has risen – someone's just blown up the Bank of England. The Prime Minister's out of the country – wouldn't it be funny if when he came back we'd all gone? Mabel's had a baby and June's had a fu-nny experience . . . just a spasm really, wasn't it, gal? I told her to put her head between her knees, but as she had a fag in her mouth at the time it did rather spoil her weekend. Still . . . Larry Grayson has been given the Queen's Award for queens. Charlie Chester has been knighted for services to literature, and Sooty has finally been swept. The cha-cha is out, the poison is in; the FT index is up and women's knickers are – ten per cent dearer than when you left [1] . . .

What else . . . ? Oh, yes, while you were away your office did very well, very well indeed . . . surprisingly well, the manager told me . . . so you needn't worry, need you? [2] Two Concordes have been sold to Rod Stewart – one for himself and the other for his singing teachers. There's a very interesting book just been published by Reader's Digest entitled, 'How I Made Love To A Polar Bear For The CIA And Found God' . . . written by John B. Dean III. Number

One in the charts is 'Highlights from Grand Opera' sung by Frankie Howerd and the big film sensation is 'The Life and Times of Mrs Mary Whitehouse,' starring Adrienne Corri and directed by Andy Warhol.

But being away is always exciting, isn't it? I went to Russia once, just a short visit. It's funny how many words in Russian seem to end in '-off' – That's one of the reasons it was only a short visit . . . In Hong Kong I had a suit made, I remember. I got back to the hotel, my pal said, 'That's nice – but what's that hump on the back?' I said, 'That's the tailor – he's still working on it . . .'

Travelling has its hazards though – just driving here to-night was touch and go. I've got this old banger, you see – no, not the wife – don't be cruel – I'm talking about my old Model T. The spark plugs won't spark, the carburettor won't carb., the battery won't batt . . . and the pistons aren't much cop either . . . And the hazards of travelling! I once spent the night in this lonely farmhouse way out on the Yorkshire moors – it was freezing cold and I had to sleep on the couch in the sitting room, because there were only the two bedrooms, the farmer and his wife in one and their 16-year-old daughter in the other. I was very uncomfortable and cold, and about two in the morning the farmer's wife – kindly old soul – crept downstairs and said, 'Would you like our eiderdown?' I said, 'No thanks, dear – she's been down twice already . . .'

Flying is the way to travel, of course. The last time I had to go to New York I went to book my seat and I said to the girl, 'How long does the flight take?' She said, 'Just a minute.' I thought 'Blimey – that's quick . . .' But what a marvellous airline – even the toilet paper was two inches wider than usual to allow for turbulence . . . It was an Italian airline – the plane had hair under the wings . . .

You were missed, Stuart, no doubt about that. But we've been practising while you were away so you'd better keep your plastic mac handy. Hope you enjoyed yourself while we were all grafting away . . . time now for you to put your nose to the wheel and your shoulders to the grindstone once again and get a twisted spine like the rest of us – Stuart: welcome home.

Suggested Headings

Homesick.

'Be it ever so humble, there's no place like home.'

Shack with nudie pix / rude hut.

Dear old face.

Changes: Philip's paying a visit to UK / Chelsea top / £'s risen – Bank of England blown up. PM's out of country / Mabel's had a baby / June a funny experience / spasm.

Larry Grayson given Queen's Award for queens.

Charlie Chester knighted for services to Literature.

Sooty has finally been swept.

Cha-cha out, the poison is in.

FT index up and women's knickers 10 per cent dearer.

While you were away your office did very well.

Two Concordes sold to Rod Stewart.

Book pub. by Reader's Digest: How I Made Love To A Polar Bear For The CIA And Found God, written by John B. Dean III.

Record. Highlights from Grand Opera / Frankie Howerd.

Film. Life And Times of Mary Whitehouse / Adrienne Corri / Andy Warhol.

Travel exciting. Russia words ending in 'off'.

Hong Kong. Suit made – hump on back.

Travelling has hazards: old banger / spark plugs / carburettor / battery / pistons.

Farmhouse on Yorkshire moors. Want eiderdown?

Flying the only way to travel. How long? Just a minute.

Toilet paper two inches wider. Italian airline.

You were missed Stuart. Keep plastic mac handy.

Enjoyed yourself? Now, nose to the wheel and shoulder to the grindstone and get a twisted spine like the rest of us.

Notes

1. This paragraph needs to be reconsidered in the light of

current events. In other words keep it topical, and, if possible, personal.

2. 'You needn't worry, need you?' should be said as though to cause the maximum worry...

3. These items also should be updated to be as topical as possible. Scan the morning's papers for possible gag material. This and the preceding paragraph should reflect as much as possible the job held by the person you are welcoming home, the place he has come from and the mode of transport.

The following may be of possible use:

The last time I went on that ferry I had one of those couchettes or whatever they're called, and in the middle of the night this girl who was in the bunk above me said, 'Are you awake?' I said, 'Yes...' She said, 'I'm cold...' I said, 'I tell you what – let's pretend we're husband and wife... just for tonight.' She said, 'All right.' I said, 'Right-oh. Get your own ruddy blanket!'

The last time I was on a plane we had serious engine trouble, so the captain said, 'We must lighten the load, so I want four volunteers to jump out. There are no parachutes, but I am sure four noble men will do this to save the other three hundred and fifty passengers.'

An Englishman – it wasn't me – immediately stood up, walked to the open door, said 'God Save the Queen,' and jumped out. A Frenchman said, 'Vive le France,' and he jumped out. Then a German said, 'Adieu, mes amis' – 'cos he could speak French, you see – and he jumped out. Then an American stood up and said, 'remember the Alamo!' and chucked a Mexican out...'

The last time I was on a plane the captain made the usual announcement but then he must have forgotten to switch the microphone off because we then all heard him say to the co-pilot, 'Do you know what I'd like now? I'd like a nice cool pint of Guinness and then I'd like to make mad, passionate love to that new, red-headed hostess.' Well, at that the hostess came rushing down the centre aisle towards the cockpit, her cheeks flaming. She got halfway along when a little old lady stopped her saying, 'You needn't rush, my dear, he's going to have his Guinness first....'

See also Farewell proposal on page 104 and Visitors proposal on page 217.

46

Welcome Home: Reply

Thank you for that applause ... for two pins I'd join in ... and thank you, Herman, for that witty and gracious speech – and so beautifully delivered. It must be wonderful being you ... yes, it's quite true – there's no humbug like home ...

I don't know whether you know this but I went to (*wherever*) for (*however long*) in order to finish a book. I'm a very slow reader ... But I did have a marvellous time there. I had a change and a rest. The hotel took my change and the taxi driver took the rest.

We just caught the train. I've found the only way to catch a train is to miss the one before. I like train journeys, though. My wife always has to sit with her back to the engine or she feels giddy and sick. I sit facing her – I've got a strong stomach. We came back in one of those Advanced Passenger Trains. Very nice and modern – and they provide little paper bags for anyone feeling a bit icky, you know. And just to help you along, inside each paper bag there's a picture of Hughie Green ... smiling [1] ...

Keeping in Britain, you don't have to worry about Customs – getting through can take an age, can't it? Last time I came through at Dover, there was this very attractive French woman in front of me and when the Customs Officer went through her case he found six pairs of panties. 'What's all this for?' he asked, and she said, 'Sunday, Monday, Tuesday, Wednesday, Thursday, Friday ...' He said, 'What about Saturday?' She said, 'Oh, Saturday – ooh la la ... !' It was a Saturday then, you see ... next was this stout motherly lady from Ramsbottom, and when the Customs officer opened her case he found twelve pairs of red flannelette draws! He said, 'What are all these, missus?' She said, 'January, February, March, April ...'

Anyway, I've got you all presents ... well, some of you

. . . well, I've got Martha a Kiss-me-Quick hat . . . second hand, I got it cheap . . . No, I'm only kidding, I've got quite a lot of presents as it happens. I went to a souvenir shop there and the chap running it asked me what I wanted, so I said, 'Quite a number of things.' He said, 'Have you got a list?' I said, 'No, I always stand like this . . .'

So for you, Mandy, there's the Magnus Pyke Book of Physical Jerks . . . For Stella there's an LP which I think she'll like – Ruby Murray's All-Time Hits . . . For young Jamie there's a do-it-yourself home vivisection kit – let him get it out of his system, mother. For Ronnie, a two-ounce tin of the local baccy . . . it's called Kerbstone Twist . . . I know you like a good shag . . . For Dad there's a new cap – with Gillette razor-blades round the peak. Dad, just the way you like it And for Mum there is that marvellous book, 'Quadratic Equations And Differential Calculus Made Fun' – it's a nice thick volume, Mum, and I thought you'd like it because it will just fit under that broken table leg in the kitchen [2] . . .

Yes, it's great to be among the old familiar faces again . . . one or two strange faces too, I see . . . mind you some of the old familiar faces are a bit strange as well . . . it's really marvellous to be back . . . (*look round with barely concealed distaste*).

At this point I was going to tell you that marvellous story about the (*whatever*) that Brian has just told . . . not the first time, Bri . . . but make sure it's the last [3] . . . So then I thought I'd tell a rather saucy story, but I thought, 'No, Mum would probably be embarrassed and Dad probably wouldn't understand it' . . . so I'll just say, thanks a million for coming to welcome me home – I'll do the same for you some day.

Suggested Headings

Thanks for applause. Two pins I'd join in.
Thanks Herman for speech. Wonderful being you.
No humbug like home.
Went to (*wherever*) to finish a book. Slow reader.

Change and rest. Hotel had change and taxi driver the rest.
Just caught the train. Miss the one before.
Wife sits with back to the engine. Giddy and sick. I sit
facing – strong stomach.
APT/paper bags/face of Hughie Green . . . smiling.
Don't have to worry about Customs.
French woman. Six pairs of panties. Stout lady. Twelve
pairs of flannelette drawers.
Presents. Martha. Kiss-me-Quick Hat. 2nd hand.
Souvenir shop. Have you a list. I always stand like this.
Mandy. Magnus Pyke Book of Physical Jerks.
Stella. LP – Ruby Murray's All-Time Hits
Jamie. Do-it-yourself home vivisection kit.
Ronnie. 2oz tin of Kerbstone Twist. Like a good shag.
Dad. New cap. Gillette blades round the peak.
Mum. Book – Quadratic Equations & Diff. Calculus Made
Fun.
Fit under broken table leg.
Old familiar faces and one or two strange faces. Great to be
back.
Was going to tell you story Brian just told about.
So saucy story. Mum embarrassed/Dad wouldn't under-
stand.
Thanks a million/do the same for you.

Notes

1. This gag can of course be altered to whatever mode of
   transport you employed. If Hughie Green is a favourite
   of yours, substitute the politician of your choice or the
   current England cricket captain – the latter will almost
   certainly be applicable to the gag (no pun intended).
2. Alter presents and recipients to suit the occasion. This is
   a popular kind of routine but it has its drawbacks – it's
   all or none, so think on before you start.
3. This to be said with comic menace in your tone and
   voice.

The following may be of possible use:

We came back by coach. Very comfortable but they had to change horses every fifteen miles.

The ship was magnificent – there were thirty-two bars ... each side! I was stopped by the police on the M6. I said, 'What's up?' The policeman said, 'Your wife fell out of the car ten miles back.' I said, 'Oh, thank goodness for that – I thought I'd gone deaf ...'

It was a good trip out but we had to wait ages for a flight showing an all-cartoon programme ... well, I like Tom and Jerry at fifteen thousand ...

See also Farewell reply on page 110 and Visitors reply on page 224.

Select Bibliography

Social customs are changing – some might say deteriorating – rapidly, and nothing is more pathetically dated than a book on speechifying or etiquette written for a pervious generation. There are surprisingly few modern books on these and allied subjects (public speaking, chairing a meeting, duties of the toast-master, etc.) and not a few of them persist in maintaining outmoded attitudes and conventions. I have therefore omitted several works normally included in a bibliography of this kind.

For further humorous stories the *Minihaha* series of small, cheap paperbacks may be of use – there are over 40 titles, 'Best Legal Jokes', 'Best Showbiz Jokes,' etc. – or the Long Laugh series by the same publisher (*Wolfe Publishing*) may cover the required field.

Works of Reference

Bartlett's Familiar Quotations
Bible Concordance
Brewer's Dictionary of Phrase and Fable
Cassell's Dictionary of Humorous Quotations
Dickens Concordance
Esar and Bentley's Treasury of Humorous Quotations
Oxford Dictionary of Quotations
Roget's Thesaurus
Shakespeare Concordance

Specific works

Andrews, Allen, Quotations for Speakers and Writers (*Newnes Books*, 1969)
Berman, Frederick, The Complete Toastmaster (*Blandford Press*, 1953)
Bullard, Audrey M., Improve Your Speech (*Anthony Blond*, 1967)

Castle, Dennis, You – As A Public Speaker (*Pelham*, 1974)

Holgate & Coulter, Speak With Confidence (*Stanley Paul*, 1974)

Kilgarriff, Michael, It Gives Me Great Pleasure (*Samuel French*, 1972)

Kilgarriff, Michael, Make 'Em Laugh (*Wolfe Publishing*, 1973)

Kilgarriff, Michael, 1,000 Jokes For Functions (*Wolfe Publishing*, 1975)

Levinson Louis, The Left Handed Dictionary (*Collier-Macmillan*, 1963)

Mackay, Colin Neil, Speak For Yourself (*Director's Bookshelf* 1971)

Norman, W. S., Etiquette and Good Manners (*EUP Teach Yourself Books*, 1962)

Palgrave, Sir Reginald, The Chairman's Handbook (*J. M. Dent & Sons*, 1964 ed)

Ward, Hazel, Social Sense and Practice (*Lutterworth Press*, 1974)

All Futura Books are available at your bookshop or newsagent, or can be ordered from the following address:
Futura Books, Cash Sales Department,
P.O. Box 11, Falmouth, Cornwall.

Please send cheque or postal order (no currency), and allow 55p for postage and packing for the first book plus 22p for the second book and 14p for each additional book ordered up to a maximum charge of £1.75 in U.K.

Customers in Eire and B.F.P.O. please allow 55p for the first book, 22p for the second book plus 14p per copy for the next 7 books, thereafter 8p per book.

Overseas customers please allow £1 for postage and packing for the first book and 25p per copy for each additional book.